CELEBRATING CHRIST'S APPEARING

The Alcuin Liturgy Guides address both practical and theoretical questions concerning the practice of worship, its setting and celebration. The Alcuin Liturgy Guides (ALG) are occasional publications alternating with major liturgical studies in a series known as the Alcuin Collections.

The first two Alcuin Liturgy Guides, *Memorial Services* by Donald Gray, and *Art and Worship* by Anne Dawtry and Christopher Irvine, were published by SPCK in 2002. ALG 3, *Celebrating the Eucharist*, by Benjamin Gordon-Taylor and Simon Jones, was published in 2005, and ALG 4, *The Use of Symbols in Worship*, edited by Christopher Irvine, was published in 2007. A complementary volume to this one (ALG 6), *Celebrating Christ's Victory*, will be published in early 2009. The series editor is the Revd Canon Christopher Irvine.

Members of the Alcuin Club receive free copies of the Collections, the Liturgy Guides, and the Joint Liturgical Studies. Founded in 1897, the Alcuin Club seeks to promote the study of Christian liturgy in general, with special reference to worship in the Anglican Communion in particular. The chairman of the Alcuin Club is the Revd Canon Dr Donald Gray CBE, and details regarding membership, the annual subscription and lists of publications can be obtained from the Secretary, Mr Jack Ryding, 'Ty Nant', 6 Parc Bach, Trefnant, Denbighshire LL16 4YE.

Visit the Alcuin Club website at **www.alcuinclub.org.uk**

CELEBRATING CHRIST'S APPEARING

Advent to Candlemas

BENJAMIN GORDON-TAYLOR
and
SIMON JONES

Alcuin Liturgy Guides 5

First published in Great Britain in 2008

Society for Promoting Christian Knowledge
36 Causton Street
London SW1P 4ST

British Library Cataloguing-in-Publication Data
A catalogue record for this book is available from the British Library

ISBN 978–0–281–05978–2

1 3 5 7 9 10 8 6 4 2

Typeset by Kenneth Burnley, Wirral, Cheshire
Printed in Great Britain by Ashford Colour Press

Produced on paper from sustainable forests

Contents

Preface

We have been most grateful for the overwhelmingly positive response to our earlier volume in this series, *Celebrating the Eucharist* (ALG 3), which seems to have met a real need among ordinands, clergy and lay leaders of worship. It seemed to us that a logical next step would be to provide guidance on the celebration of the liturgical year, and the result is this volume and its companion (ALG 6: *Celebrating Christ's Victory*). As ever, we have been blessed with the advice and encouragement of many colleagues, students and friends, not least the series editor, Canon Christopher Irvine, and our colleagues and students at Mirfield and in Oxford, to all of whom we offer our sincere thanks.

B.G.-T.
S.M.J.

Abbreviations

ASB	*The Alternative Service Book 1980.*
BCP	The Book of Common Prayer 1662.
CCW1	Paul Bradshaw, *Companion to Common Worship* Vol. 1.
CCW2	Paul Bradshaw, *Companion to Common Worship* Vol. 2.
CF	*Common Worship: Festivals.*
CI	*Common Worship: Christian Initiation.*
CLC	*The Christian Year: Calendar, Lectionary and Collects.*
CW	*Common Worship.*
CWMV	*Common Worship: Services and Prayers for the Church of England* [= Common Worship 'Main Volume'].
DP	*Common Worship: Daily Prayer.*
GIRM	*General Instruction of the Roman Missal.*
LHWE	*Lent, Holy Week, Easter: Services and Prayers.*
NEH	*The New English Hymnal.*
PE	*Common Worship: President's Edition.*
PHG	*The Promise of His Glory: Services and Prayers for the Season from All Saints to Candlemas.*
PS	*Common Worship: Pastoral Services.*
TS	*Common Worship: Times and Seasons.*
WM	*The Weekday Missal.*

1

Introduction

Our earlier volume in this series, *Celebrating the Eucharist* (ALG 3), belongs to a distinct genre of liturgical manual. Material which has sought to explain, direct and guide the celebration of the Eucharist from the particular point of view of the president is plentiful. For the celebration of the seasons and feasts of the liturgical year, however, there are fewer works which seek to cover the whole year. Some of those that do are mainly concerned with the Eucharist in its various forms; they include classic works to which we referred in ALG 3 such as *Ritual Notes* and Fortescue and O'Connell, *Ceremonies of the Roman Rite Described.* In these, however, may also be found the unique ceremonial for the great seasons as celebrated in the Roman Catholic Church before the Second Vatican Council and in some communities in the Church of England, particularly before the process of liturgical reform which resulted in the Alternative Service Book (hereafter ASB) got under way. In some places this ceremonial is to some degree still used, particularly where the rites are celebrated in traditional language, perhaps using some texts from the *English Missal.* These earlier forms are part of the process of liturgical evolution, and most parishes and other communities which celebrate the liturgical year corporately now do so according to more recent revisions of the rites, Roman and Anglican.

Many in the Church of England rediscovered the riches of the liturgical year with the help and inspiration of such publications as *Holy Week Services* by the Joint Liturgical Group (1971), *Lent, Holy Week, Easter* (1986) (hereafter LHWE) and *The Promise of His Glory* (1991) (hereafter PHG). These communities and still others are now seeking to become familiar with the plentiful resources of the latest stage of evolution in the Church of England, *Common Worship: Times and Seasons* (2006) (hereafter TS). The Roman Rite in its modern form continues to supplement these resources, and in some communities provides the majority of the texts.

Assistance with the interpretation and use of the newer versions of the ancient rites is present to a degree in the publications themselves, more so than ever before in TS. There have also been separate guides, some of which concentrate on history and text, others including some ceremonial guidance also. Examples are the volumes by Michael Perham and Kenneth Stevenson which accompanied LHWE and PHG, entitled *Waiting for the Risen Christ* (1986) and *Welcoming the Light of Christ* (1991) respectively. Various publications in the *Using Common Worship* series (Church House Publishing/Praxis) and the *Worship* series of Grove Books have covered individual occasions or whole seasons, but have tended to concentrate on the selection of texts, giving less space to the ceremonial expression of the rites. This is not to suggest too sharp a division between text and action but to point to the importance of the manner of their necessary interaction.

Less common, then, have been publications which have ceremonial as their starting point, assuming that interaction with text will itself be part of the liturgical action as a whole. Nor are there many which seek to cover in a relatively short space the whole liturgical year. In 1930 the Alcuin Club published *A Directory of Ceremonial: Part II (Seasons)* (Alcuin Club Tracts XIX), but it is relatively limited in scope. Of more recent volumes, Mgr Peter Elliott's *Ceremonies of the Liturgical Year According to the Roman Rite* (2002) is a notable example in the Roman tradition. The present volume and the next in the Alcuin Liturgy Guides series attempt to redress this mainly with the rites and texts contained in TS and *Common Worship: Festivals* (hereafter CF) in mind, although as with the earlier guide to the Eucharist, we shall have an eye to the wider Western tradition also. In what is offered here we have quite freely and openly drawn on the commentary on TS, written by one of us, to be found in *Companion to Common Worship*, Vol. 2, but have sought to address more practical issues. For detailed information as to the sources of particular texts, the reader is directed to that commentary.

In seeking to give guidance for the celebration of the liturgical year we hope to convey a sense of its sheer importance, that parishes and other communities will take full advantage of the possibilities offered by current resources. We will give most space to the most solemn and joyful occasions, such as the rites of Holy Week and the Christmas–Epiphany cycle, but it must not be forgotten that in the liturgical year as a whole is encountered the single mystery of God in Christ, the particular occasions being lenses through which it is viewed and points of encounter with its dynamic, transforming reality. The significance of individual saints' days must not be underestimated in this, in the sense that they may be seen in proper perspective precisely in relation to those occasions which celebrate the great events of the saving mysteries, on account of which martyrs died, doctors taught and missionaries preached. A joyful celebration of Easter, then, is continued in the marking of the life and ministry of those whose whole purpose was the preaching of the cross and resurrection. The Church continues to do this individually and corporately, inspired by the saints and participating in the liturgical encounter with the reality of the saving mysteries, every time the word is proclaimed and the sacraments celebrated. In attempting to give guidance for the celebration of seasons and principal feasts we are implicitly drawing attention to the importance of the year as a whole in its richness and in its simplicity, not necessarily opposed, both of which may have a part to play on a single occasion.

In ALG 3 we drew attention to the importance of liturgy as 'text in performance', and we would wish to re-emphasize that here. Many of the issues surrounding liturgical style in Chapter 1 of *Celebrating the Eucharist* are also relevant to the present context, as are the remarks on liturgical space and particular ministries in Chapter 2 of that volume.

The liturgical year

The advent of the third millennium has drawn attention to the human fascination with time, and the calendar as a means of giving it order and structure has also been the subject of popular interest. The Christian understanding of time is grounded in the Hebrew Scriptures, and their interpretative accounts of the intervention of God in human history. Key events in this history, such as the Exodus, became occasions of regular celebration, but not only in terms of remembering, and certainly not in the form of dry historical re-enactment. Instead, they were occasions of shared celebration of and commitment to the involvement of God in the life of the community of his chosen. The Christian community has also ordered time in a way that expresses belief in God as Lord of time, although there have been differences of theological emphasis and liturgical expression. The Christian calendar is therefore an interface between God and Church, and between Church and world. Deliberately linked to the lectionary, it is also an interface between Bible and Church. The Christian ordering of time is therefore something dynamic, not lifeless or mechanistic. Nor need its liturgical celebration be seen any longer as the preserve of a particular theological tradition.

Participation in the Christian year is not simply a pious historical reflection on the life and acts of Jesus Christ, but a celebration of the one mystery of God in Christ which allows the Christ of faith to grow in us and in the Church. It is a celebration not of what Christ did or said, but of Christ himself. The mystery is accessible to us through many different lenses, whether in scripture or in the sacramental life of the Church and of our daily lives. We cannot yet acknowledge its entirety. We celebrate the saving acts of Christ because we are not yet whole, but seek to be so through his mercy and love. Each season and festival is a window onto God, a view through a glass darkly, and the celebration of each an aspiration to see him face to face. In the words of Thomas Merton, liturgical time is 'humanly insecure, seeking its peace altogether outside the structures of all that is established, visible and familiar, in the shape of a kingdom which is not seen' (Merton 1976: p. 40).

Beyond human attempts to divide up and organize it, time is *already* hallowed, because God is Lord of history and creator of all that we experience. Thus Aidan Kavanagh's insight that for Jews and Christians the meaning of time is found in the self-revelation of the creator, and that consequently time is not merely sequential, a 'succession of bare moments', but also 'a powerful thrust home toward its holy source'. This means, he says, 'that the liturgy needs time rather than time needs liturgy' (Kavanagh 1992: p. 24). Much earlier, and in the Anglican context, Richard Hooker could declare:

> As the substance of God alone is infinite and hath *no kind* of limitation, so likewise his continuance is from everlasting to everlasting and knoweth neither beginning nor end. Which demonstrable conclusion being presupposed, it followeth necessarily that besides him all things are finite both in substance and in continuance.
>
> (Hooker 1890: vol. 2)

The Church and its liturgy are inseparable from what Hooker, in the same place, calls the 'infinite continuance of God'.

The relationship between time and the liturgy speaks of 'the divine saving presence' as the source of ultimate meaning (Cooke 1990: p. 1116) including the ultimate meaning of time as 'a purposeful thrust home toward its holy source', to repeat Kavanagh. In this sense, the calendar is not just a historical association of events in sequence, but its celebration is to participate in something which points to the self-revelation of God. Furthermore, it makes this self-revelation present to us and ourselves present to it.

Odo Casel (1886–1948), the influential Benedictine liturgist, saw that the liturgical year should not simply be seen as a series of commemorations, 'not a gradual unfolding in the sense that the year of nature develops', but something which makes present 'a single divine act which demands and finds gradual accustoming on [our] part, though in itself complete'. On each feast and in each season, 'the entire saving mystery' is before us, and 'more concretely on each occasion'. Advent and Lent typify the fact that there is no time of the year in which the *entire* mystery is not present. For example: 'We celebrate Advent, not by putting ourselves back into the state of unredeemed mankind, but in the certainty of the Lord who has already appeared to us, for whom we must prepare our souls' (Casel 1962: pp. 66–8).

Casel is essentially reformulating an idea already present in the preaching of Bernard of Clairvaux. For Bernard, Advent is a season with both the first and second comings of Christ in view, with a third between them, 'wherein those who know the Lord sleep with great delight', encountering the presence of Christ with his people here and now in sacramental signs. The effect of this 'intermediate' coming of the Lord is the renewal of the soul:

> As long as earthly bread is in the bin, a thief can steal it, or a mouse can gnaw it, or it can go mouldy. But once you have eaten it, what then have you to fear from mould or mouse or thief? Even so guard the Word of God, for blessed are they that keep it. Transfer it to the stomach of your soul; let it pass over into your affections and behaviour.
>
> (Bernard of Clairvaux, *De Adventu Domini*, V, 1–3)

Thomas Merton, who loved Bernard, made a study of his Advent writings very explicitly entitled 'The Sacrament of Advent in the Spirituality of St Bernard', in which he concludes that for Bernard

> . . . the Sacrament (of Advent) is the *Presence of Christ in the world* as Savior. In his theology Advent does not merely commemorate the Incarnation as a historical event, nor is it a mere devotional preparation for the Feast of Christmas, nor an anticipation of the Last Judgment. It is above all the 'sacrament' of the Presence of God in the world and in time in His Incarnate Word, in His Kingdom, above all His presence in *our own* lives as *our* Savior. The sacrament of Advent is the *necessaria praesentia Christi* [the needful presence of Christ].
>
> (Merton 1965: p. 64, quoting Bernard, *Homilia*, VII, ii)

Advent is used here as an example of principles that may be applied to the Christian year as a whole. In Casel's understanding and, by inference, in wider thought, the Paschal Mystery even in extended, humanly organized temporal celebration, is one and undivided. It is present in the reality of Christ at all times and in all places as the consequence of Easter and the ascension. Casel likens the liturgical year to the action of a screw thread: each successive celebration spirals ever upwards: there is nothing new in successive years; we already know what it contains and that it will come round again, but each celebration of it brings the Church nearer to the *eschaton*, deeper into the mystery of salvation (Casel 1941: p. 7). In the words of Noële Denis-Boulet, 'just as the sacraments contain and effect what they signify, so the Christian year, in respect of the eternity of grace, is the image and ever-repeated manifestation of the Redeemer-God in our lives'. As the redeeming work of Christ is the primordial mystery, the liturgical year which 'makes it actual and human' is itself 'a derived mystery and a kind of sacrament in the wider sense' (Denis-Boulet 1960: pp. 120–1).

In the early centuries of the evolution of the calendar there is to be seen emerging a tension between a historical and an eschatological emphasis that is still present in it today and is of positive and creative value. Another creative tension is twofold, and concerns the commemoration of the saints. The first element of this concerns a cycle of fixed dates in relation to a cycle of moveable seasons – the *Sanctorale* in relation to the *Temporale*. The second element is the life of humanity in relation to the life of heaven.

The first element may seem to suggest that this is a question of reconciling the simultaneous operation of two conflicting systems – it would be entirely and typically human to wish this to happen. After all, it may seem that the seasons have a habit of getting in the way of the observance of saints' days. Indeed, such has been the concern to emphasize the primacy of the seasons that the *Sanctorale* has always been at the mercy of the liturgical blue pencil. For instance, the liturgical implementation of Vatican II included a drastic cull of saints, particularly those of dubious reputation or existence, but partly also to avoid the fact that almost every day of the year directed the commemoration of at least one saint, which was rightly deemed to be particularly unhelpful in Advent, Lent and the Easter season. The English Prayer Books had done the same thing in the sixteenth centuries but for different reasons. It was never true that Anglican theology had no interest in calendrical matters, however. We have already encountered Richard Hooker in this respect, and there is of course the corpus of liturgical preaching by such great figures as the Bishops Lancelot Andrewes and John Cosin. None directly addresses the issue of the *Temporale* and *Sanctorale* in tension, but a magnificent poem by John Donne suggests that reconciliation of the two is not the point, and that it is in the very tension that the sacramental activity of God may best be seen. It happens every so often that the date of the Annunciation falls on Good Friday. It happened in 1608, and the result was the poem 'Upon the Annunciation and Passion falling upon one day':

> Shee sees him man, so like God made in this,
> That of them both a circle emblem is,
> Whose first and last concur; this doubtful day
> Of feast or fast, Christ came, and went away.

Having thus set up the tension, Donne explores its implications:

> At once a Son is promis'd her, and gone,
> Gabriel gives Christ to her, He her to John;
> Not fully a mother, Shee's in Orbity,
> At once receiver and the legacy.
> All this, and all between, this day hath shown,
> Th'Abridgement of Christ's story, which makes one
> (As in plain Maps, the furthest West is East)
> Of the Angel's *Ave*, and *Consummatum est.*

Nevertheless, it is a matter of rejoicing that such an apparently infelicitous collision of theological turning-points occasionally happens, and important that it is rare:

> How well the Church, God's court of faculties
> Deals, in some times, and seldom joining these!

For Donne, the point is that the occurrence emphasizes the unity of what Christ achieves, and by implication its presence for the Church in the liturgy. By overlaying the incarnation with the crucifixion, in merging feast and fast, fixed date and moveable observance, a greater insight is gained into the activity of God in creation and among his people – a sacramental activity in which, by the grace of God, outward form points to hidden mystery. Therefore, Donne continues,

> This Church, by letting these days join, hath shown
> Death and conception in mankind is one.

This single example from the seventeenth century shows how season and festival are joined in ways far more significant than the superficial incompatibilities of their co-existence. This is no argument for abandoning the transferring of feasts, but there is shown by this one happy collision that the calendar in its temporal and sanctoral aspects has a dynamism which is itself in tension with human systems of order and time. The dynamism results from the fact that God is involved – it is a consequence of the incarnation, and is vivified by the passion, resurrection and ascension.

The second element is the tension in the saints between humanity and the life of heaven. Once more, this is precisely the point, if only because it is in some sense a reflection of the nature of Christ himself. More than this, they typify the redeeming work of Christ and the work of his Spirit in men and women throughout history. Christ is the personification of the mystery spoken of in the Letter to the Ephesians:

> He has made known to us in all wisdom and insight the mystery of his will, according to his purpose set forth in Christ as a plan for the fullness of time, to unite all things in him, things in heaven and things on earth.
>
> (Ephesians 1.9–10)

So the saints as examples of redeemed humanity are images, a series of lenses through which that single mystery of God in Christ is seen and made present. The historical record is not the only purpose, or even the principal one. The *Sanctorale* is, as Patrick Cowley notes,

> much more than a mere roll of honour, and its day by day observance is not only a pious recollection of historic events and people . . . It perpetuates the past into the present, and, in one sense, makes all contemporary.
>
> (Cowley 1960: p. 12)

It is 'sacramental' in this sense of transcending time in that the grace given to the saints is available to the Church of the present. The saints proclaim the possibility of redemption as well as its achievement, and so their 'yearly remembrance', a phrase which recurs in many collects, is an *anamnesis* of a nature akin to that of the Eucharist in that it makes present in reality and newness, but not of course repetition, what Christ did in his holy ones, and so strengthens the Church and gives it hope. The *Sanctorale* is therefore sacramental in this sense also: the fruits of martyrdom, for example, become part of the rich outpouring of grace which the sacramental relationship of God and the world entails, and are thus as much 'now' as they were 'then' in historical time. As Cowley further states, 'The Church sees in the saints the reality of the conquest of Christ over sinful human nature and the highest justification of all Christian assertions' (Cowley 1960: p. 14).

The tensions in the history and the theology of the calendar are thus in fact part of its nature and purpose. These tensions form the basis of a sacramental understanding of the calendar as an aspect of the liturgy which is dynamic and alive, despite its susceptibility to rules and the printed page. Such an understanding is vital. The calendar conveys both the history of God's activity as Lord of history, and the present reality of the presence of Christ in the Church. To borrow language from biblical studies, it is part of the liturgical *bricolage* of the Church, and has a polyvalence that enables it to burst the chains of a rigid notion of time. The humanly fashioned tomb could not hold Christ: so humanly conceived time cannot contain his activity.

The liturgical year in the Church of England

The Christian calendar, of which the *Common Worship* (hereafter CW) calendar is the latest form in the Church of England, consists of two overall cycles, customarily known as the *Temporale* and the *Sanctorale*. *Temporale*, as the Latin implies, refers to the course of times and seasons of the year, such as Advent, Easter, and what several traditions now call 'Ordinary Time', that is a period when no other season is being observed. The *Sanctorale*, as the word also implies, is the particular choice and sequence of saints' days through the year. In the Anglican tradition these are often referred to as 'Red Letter' days (the principal celebrations), and 'Black Letter' days (the lesser observances), terms originating from the colours in which these categories of observance appeared in printed calendars in liturgical books, a custom which survives in some books.

The 1549 Prayer Book and its successors sought to simplify the liturgical year, with a drastic reduction in associated ceremonies and variable seasonal texts such as proper prefaces to the Eucharistic Prayer and proper collects and readings. What came to be known as 'Black Letter' saints' days had no provision of proper texts, and may have been included only to assist in the calculation of secular dates. The proposed 1927/8 revision retained the basic pattern of seasons and major festivals with some minor adjustments and improvements, such as the elevation of the transfiguration (6 August) to the status of a Red Letter day with its own proper texts, and the provision of more proper prefaces. There was, by now, a conscious intention to celebrate Black Letter days, and these were given common texts according to category. More controversially, an explicit 'Commemoration of All Souls' was restored on 2 November, indicating greater doctrinal breadth in the Church of England by this time, which in the matter of prayer for the departed was greatly influenced by the experience of the First World War.

The formation of the Liturgical Commission in the 1950s led to a further re-examination of the criteria for inclusion in the *Sanctorale*, and ultimately to the work which resulted in the calendar of ASB. Here, for the first time in an authorized calendar, post-Reformation figures were added, and a more radical approach taken to the seasons, this time interlocking with the new two-year lectionary which began the Christian year on the Ninth Sunday before Christmas and entitled the Sundays of what is now the second period of 'Ordinary Time' Sundays 'after Pentecost'. The subsequent 'commended' material in LHWE and PHG indicated a desire to encourage a still richer observance of the seasons and feasts of the liturgical year, and the latter laid the foundations for some of the features now included in the latest revision.

The *Common Worship* calendar

To accompany the revised calendar of the Church of England, the Liturgical Commission itself provided notes and a commentary in the first published edition of 1997, *Calendar, Lectionary and Collects* (hereafter CLC). It is significant that the Notes to the calendar begin with a comment on Sundays which declares: 'All Sundays celebrate the paschal mystery of the death and resurrection of the Lord' (CLC: p. 10). The calendar is an aspect of the Church's call to celebration, not merely a lifeless structure. All Christian celebration is grounded in the Paschal Mystery, and this mystery historically and theologically finds its focus on Sunday. Thus the CW calendar is placed firmly in the contemporary understanding of liturgical time, whereby the historical, the christological and the eschatological aspects of Christian celebration may be seen as a coherent whole, with no exclusive emphasis, but still reflecting in the seasons and feasts different aspects of the one mystery of God in Christ. TS sets out the CW scheme in the Rules to Order the Christian Year (pp. 24–30), including Liturgical Colours (p. 29) and a Table of Transferences (p. 30).

Classification and terminology

Compared to the Book of Common Prayer, the system of classifying and naming feast days in the Church of England has become more complex in recent years, although not nearly as complex as that of the old Roman calendar as described by Fortescue and O'Connell and as imitated by *Ritual Notes*, compared to which the modern Roman system is simplicity itself. In descending order of importance, CW calls liturgical observances Principal Feasts, Principal Holy Days, Festivals, Lesser Festivals and Commemorations. To avoid confusion it should be noticed that the number of categories has expanded since ASB, and equivalent ranks have been given new names. 'Principal Holy Day' in ASB becomes 'Principal Feast', and 'Principal Holy Day' is used in the CW calendar only to denote Ash Wednesday, Maundy Thursday and Good Friday. The 'Festivals and Greater Holy Days' in ASB, which included these three occasions, now no longer do so and are simply 'Festivals'. CW distinguishes between 'Lesser Festivals' and 'Commemorations'. ASB made the briefest of mentions of local celebrations, but CW gives much more explicit encouragement to local *Sanctorales* and the celebration of Dedication and Patronal Festivals.

Many communities and individuals will also be familiar with the Roman Catholic terminology, which corresponds to that of CW (see Table 1).

Observances common to both calendars are not necessarily of the equivalent rank, nor do they necessarily share the same name, although it is common for the Roman Catholic names of certain observances to be adopted locally.

Principal Feasts

Called Principal Holy Days in ASB, in CW these are Christmas Day, Epiphany, the Presentation of Christ in the Temple (Candlemas), the Annunciation, Easter Day, Ascension Day, Pentecost, Trinity Sunday

Table 1 ASB, CW and RC terminology

ASB term	*CW term*	*RC term*
Principal Holy Day	**Principal Feast**	Solemnity
Greater Holy Day	**Principal Holy Day**	*No term*
Festival	**Festival**	Feast
Lesser Festival and Commemoration	**Lesser Festival**	Memoria
	Commemoration	Optional Memoria

and All Saints' Day. These additions partly reflect a more developed approach to the seasons: the Presentation is encouraged as a more appropriate end of the season of Christmas, Sundays in the second period of 'Ordinary Time' are 'after Trinity' rather than 'after Pentecost', and All Saintstide is given more significance, following the lead given in PHG. Principal Feasts take precedence over any other observance, although the Annunciation must be transferred where it falls in Holy Week or Easter Week; and Epiphany, the Presentation and All Saints may be transferred for pastoral reasons to the nearest Sunday, as TS explains (p. 30). This does not apply to Christmas Day or Ascension Day, which must be kept on the specific day, although the Roman Catholic Church in England and Wales has recently and controversially permitted the transfer of the Ascension to the following Sunday. CW does not allow this.

Principal Holy Days

Ash Wednesday, Maundy Thursday and Good Friday are the only three Principal Holy Days, as they do not have a festal character (with the possible exception of Maundy Thursday in its Eucharistic aspect and in that *Gloria in Excelsis* is sung), but have a status which precludes any other observance.

Festivals

In ASB these were also called 'Greater Holy Days'. This confusion has now been removed, and some changes made to the list in order to resolve anomalies or respond to inter-Anglican, ecumenical and other interests. The Naming of Jesus *or* The Circumcision of Christ is now The Naming and Circumcision of Jesus (1 January). George is included as Patron of England (23 April). Following the Revised Common Lectionary and ecumenical Western practice, Christ the King is celebrated on the Sunday before Advent. The main festival of the Blessed Virgin Mary is moved to 15 August, thus bringing it into line with most other Anglican provinces and wider ecumenical practice, although the Commission is careful to point out that controversial doctrinal implications should not be inferred from this, and the option remains to keep it on 8 September, as in ASB. The Visit of the Blessed Virgin Mary to Elizabeth (31 May) and Holy Cross Day (14 September) are now kept as festivals. The common alternative title for the Day of Thanksgiving for the Holy Communion, Corpus Christi, is acknowledged, and it may be kept as a Festival on the Thursday after Trinity Sunday, a recognition of the existing practice of some communities.

Lesser Festivals and Commemorations

While the Lesser Festivals are intended to include the majority of those feasts which occur on weekdays, they are nevertheless to be 'observed at the level appropriate to a particular church' (TS: p. 28). Several additions have been made to those included in ASB, the rationale for which is helpfully set out in the Commission's commentary in CLC (pp. 245–6). The Commemorations are intended to be of less importance liturgically, but may still be celebrated as Lesser Festivals if local circumstances suggest it. Overall, the CW *Sanctorale* does much to bring into the ambit of the liturgy figures whose contribution and witness have not necessarily been exclusively Anglican or indeed in England, thus reflecting ecumenical appreciation and the increasingly international character of Anglicanism. This has been given striking visual form at Westminster Abbey by the installation of the statues of six twentieth-century martyrs. During the seasons care must be taken when selecting which Lesser Festivals and Commemorations to observe, and how to observe them, to avoid excessively obscuring the character of the season. Suggestions to assist with this are made in discussing the relevant seasons in this Guide and in ALG 6.

Sundays

Each Sunday celebrates the resurrection in whichever season it occurs as well as in Ordinary Time. However, a Festival which falls on a Sunday may be celebrated on the First or Second Sunday of Christmas, a Sunday of Epiphany, a Sunday before Lent, a Sunday after Trinity and a Sunday before Advent, although transferring it to the nearest free weekday is a permitted alternative (see TS: p. 24). No Festival may be observed on a Sunday in Advent, Lent or Eastertide.

The seasons

Particular emphasis is properly given to Eastertide as a season of primary importance. The Paschal character of Eastertide ought to offer at least as much rich possibility in scripture and liturgical celebration as Advent, Christmas, Epiphany and Lent. To reflect this, Sundays in Eastertide are 'of Easter' rather than 'after'; therefore the former 'First Sunday after Easter' (Low Sunday) is now the 'Second Sunday of Easter'. During Eastertide no Festival may be celebrated on a Sunday unless it is the Patronal or Dedication Festival of a Church, and even then consideration should be given to celebrating these on the nearest available weekday. In Easter Week no Festival, Lesser Festival or Commemoration may be observed.

CW does not follow PHG in having a 'Kingdom' season between All Saints and Advent, although the lectionary does reflect on the reign of Christ during this period. Instead, the period after All Saints is one of remembrance of the saints, and the option is given of using red as the liturgical colour during this time, although without historical precedent. Advent Sunday has been restored in CW to its proper status as the beginning of the liturgical year, and is also, of course, the day on which the lectionary year changes.

Outside the seasons, the title 'Ordinary Time' is used to refer to the period between the Presentation and Lent, and the period of 'Sundays after Trinity'. This has been the subject of discussion focusing on the appropriateness of the word 'Ordinary' in the context of Christian worship. However, in actual fact, each Sunday may be called by a number of different names according to choice. This partly results from the differing terminologies employed by the calendar and the lectionary, and the fact that the cycle of readings in Ordinary Time is calculated independently of the title of the Sunday. It will therefore be up to each community to decide how these names are to be used, but priority should be given to emphasizing the seasons, and to the 'after Trinity' label, in order to avoid the sense that some Sundays of the year are somehow of less importance or interest.

Additional to the above are Days of Discipline and Self Denial, and Ember Days, continuing the tradition of BCP and ASB in identifying these occasions. There are also, of course, many themes officially, semi-officially or unofficially associated with particular

Sundays, for example Mothering Sunday, Remembrance Sunday, Bible Sunday, Education Sunday, and Sea Sunday. CW provides prayers and readings for some of these.

Liturgical colours

More detailed consideration of the colours for particular seasons or occasions will be found in the relevant sections in this Guide and in ALG 6. Generally speaking, however, the visual dimension which they enhance should not be underestimated. The *General Instruction of the Roman Missal* (hereafter GIRM) declares liturgical colours to give 'effective expression even outwardly to the specific character of the mysteries of faith being celebrated and to a sense of Christian life's passage through the course of the liturgical year' (GIRM: s. 345). In this sense, liturgical colours are an aspect of the common pilgrimage of the Church in response to God's call, and the pilgrimage of the individual towards spiritual growth and maturity. Colour is an aspect of creation, a gift to the senses which assists the human capacity to encounter beauty and see in it the hand of the creator. It therefore has a place in worship, where the response of creation to the creator is typically expressed. This means that where liturgical colours are used, careful consideration should be given to their context and quality, lest they become an empty piece of ritual.

Liturgical revision in the Church of England has made official a recognition of liturgical colours that was already present in older works of liturgical history and manuals of liturgical practice. Percy Dearmer, for instance, devotes considerable space to colours in his *Parson's Handbook*. Revision has encouraged simplification of what grew into a complex scheme in the Middle Ages. It is worth noting this earlier complexity, however, for it suggests a rich visual dimension that contemporary liturgy ought not to ignore, and indeed some have interpreted this as a dimension of freedom of practice rather than as a rigid system, the latter ironically coming later to the detriment of local variety. Thus Dearmer explains and laments:

> Liturgical colours may be said to have reached their most elaborate development in France and Spain . . . where the colour customs of the cathedral churches were developed and systematized for diocesan use

> with great elaboration, only, alas! to succumb to ultramontane uniformity.
>
> (Dearmer 1932: p. 103)

Dearmer was mostly concerned with 'What' rather than 'Why', yet he comments that in England, 'there seems to have been great freedom of practice', and indeed the older tradition does contain some sensible advice that is still valuable and which, with imagination, might form part of contemporary usage. This is seen, for example, in the medieval English practice that the best vesture of whatever colour should be used on the most solemn feasts, the offering of the best of the work of human hands in the service of worship being more important than its particular colour – a principle actually adopted in modern times by the then new Liverpool Cathedral (see Dearmer 1932: p. 115). There were presumably limits: even a very fine black and gold cope would not be suitable for Easter Day, but a red and gold one would be entirely appropriate according to this principle. Churches which possess relatively little in the way of vestments may well find encouragement in such things. Dearmer (p. 116) suggests what may even now seem to be a radical simplification based on his interpretation of 'English' usage:

Festivals:	The best materials
Lent:	The Lenten White
Other Days:	Any other materials

but this may be taking things too far, and of course the Church of England has very generally adopted most aspects of the Roman scheme in its official advice, although 'Lent array' and 'Advent blue' do feature in some places. The point is surely that there is some rationale arising from liturgical principles rather than personal taste or random whim, and it is this sort of informed decision that we here encourage.

The CW scheme with its alternatives is given in TS (p. 29). The 'default' pattern is relatively simple and comprises white, red, purple and green. However, these are 'not mandatory and traditional or local use may be followed'. More detail on instances where changes to the default scheme may be considered will be found in the relevant section in this guide and ALG 6, but a summary of the default colours and possible alternatives for various possible calendrical and pastoral occasions is given in Table 2.

The alternatives make for a surprisingly complex scheme, so care must be taken in making choices. While it is quite sufficient to stick to the main sequence shown in bold type in Table 2, the possible variations offer teaching opportunities and expression of local culture.

Some churches have adopted 'year round' vestments and hangings, or sometimes only for the principal altar. As the term suggests, these are made up of a mixture of colours and perhaps symbols not connected with a particular season, although the base is often white. While money may be saved, the variety of the colours and the liturgical significance of their changing will be lost. Liturgical colours are not merely decorative, but form part of the symbolic architecture of liturgical celebration.

Table 2 Default colours and alternatives for various occasions

Occasion	*Default colour*	*Alternative colour*	*Occasion*
Christmas, Epiphany, Easter, Trinity, Saints (not Martyrs), Initiation, Marriage, Ordination	**White**	Gold	Principal Feast
		Red	Initiation, Ordination
		Purple	Funeral (except of a child)
		Black	Funeral (except of a child)
Holy Week, Martyrs, Pentecost	**Red**	Green	All Saints to eve of Advent
Advent, Lent, Funeral	**Purple**	Roman purple	Lent
		Violet	Advent
		Blue	Advent or Lent
		Black	Funeral, All Souls
		White	Funeral, All Souls
		Unbleached linen	Lent
		Rose	Advent 3, Lent 4
Ordinary Time	**Green**	Red	All Saints to eve of Advent

Processions

Processions form part of several seasonal liturgies, and so it may be found helpful to give some general principles here. They formed a distinctive and increasingly elaborate part of medieval liturgy in England, but this does not imply the need for a renewed liturgical archaeology. The Alcuin Club published Colin Dunlop's *Processions: A Dissertation Together with Practical Suggestions* as Alcuin Club Tracts XX in 1932, and it is worth repeating the following sensible words from the first chapter:

> . . . the aim is to discover briefly the motives which lie behind the Procession as an act of worship, to note what historically have been its main features; and then to try, with the help of the principles thus collected, to reconstruct the Procession as a liturgical means of leading modern congregations into a more ready understanding of the Christian faith, and of expressing less remotely some of their religious aspirations. It is not the main aim of this book to give directions for the carrying out in modern churches of the exact or even of the adapted ceremonial of the medieval services . . . Here the attempt is to understand what instincts prompted such Processions in the past, and to give those same instincts a ready means of expression in a variety of ways today.
>
> (Dunlop 1932: p. 9)

Here indeed we intend a still more practical than historical emphasis, and two further principles of Dunlop's work which still hold good are that a procession is an act of worship, and that it has the potential to enrich the liturgy and understanding of it. The processions which may accompany particular liturgical occasions in the year must serve to deepen appreciation of the significance of those occasions. In other words, processions are not a form of entertainment, and yet they can be moving in both physical and spiritual terms and evocative of a characteristic of life with God – the Christian journey. An additional characteristic of the procession is not merely liturgical – a procession is an act of witness to the gospel, as is often explicitly the case on Good Friday where an outdoor, often ecumenical procession is made, and at Corpus Christi where an outdoor procession of the Blessed Sacrament is the custom. The procession is therefore an intersection of liturgy and mission, in whatever form it takes, as well as a sign of the Church in pilgrimage. George Herbert, typically, finds in the procession associated with the beating of parish bounds some important principles, or 'advantages' as he calls them. He writes in *A Priest to the Temple*:

> Particularly [the country Parson] loves Procession, and maintains it, because there are contained therein four manifest advantages. First, a blessing of God for the fruits of the field: Secondly, justice in the Preservation of bounds: Thirdly, Charity in loving walking, and neighbourly accompanying one another, with reconciling of differences at that time, if there be any: Fourthly, Mercy in relieving the poor by a liberal distribution and largesse, which at that time is or ought to be used.
>
> (Hutchinson 1941: p. 284)

The third of these is a beautiful image: the notion that the priest and community share in a 'loving walk' which both *binds* them as humans in Christ and which gives opportunity for *freedom* from the *bonds* of disagreement, 'if', as Herbert hopefully says, 'there be any'. In the marking in procession of the physical bounds of the parish is found the enacted proclamation of the gospel and the visible manifestation of the Church in pilgrimage.

The practicalities of processions will vary according to the nature of a liturgical space, local geography and local custom. Details for the liturgical requirements of the various processions in the liturgical year will be found in the appropriate section of this guide and its companion ALG 6. A general remark which may be made, however, is that people often seem reluctant to process or are restrained in their processing, whatever the occasion. There must be order in a liturgical procession which includes the entire assembly, and a concern for safety if it involves using local roads (in which case a large event must involve liaison with the police). But there is no need for a procession to be excessively regimented, although it may be solemn or joyous: people should not necessarily feel compelled to walk in neat pairs, although this can naturally result from confined spaces such as narrow aisles. Ultimately it will be for each community to find the right 'level' for each occasion.

* * *

In the following chapters we will deal with the liturgies of Advent, Christmas, Epiphany, The Presentation of Christ, and All Saints to Advent, in that order. The final chapter concerns the use of the CW Daily Prayer and Initiation material in respect of the seasons of the liturgical year, and as such covers the whole year. ALG 6, *Celebrating Christ's Victory*, will complete the year in detail and also make some comment on the material in TS for Seasons and Festivals of the Agricultural Year.

2

Advent

And now we give you thanks
because you sent him to redeem us from sin and death,
  and to make us inheritors of eternal life;
that when he shall come again in power and great triumph
  to judge the world,
we may with joy behold his appearing,
and in confidence may stand before him.
(Short Preface for Advent, TS: p. 39)

Liturgical character

Is Advent a penitential or preparatory season? It has often been thought of as a 'little Lent'. This was one emphasis in the tradition, but preparation is another, and more important to the extent that older liturgical manuals categorically dismiss Advent as a penitential season, although not unanimously. In *Ritual Notes*, Fortescue and O'Connell and Dearmer rule out penitence as a controlling theme. For example:

> The tendency of the present day to make another Lent of Advent is much to be deprecated. The *O Sapientia* [the first of the Great O Antiphons] in our Kalendar and the use of Sequences in the old English books may remind us of the spirit of joyful expectation which is the liturgical characteristic of Advent.
>
> (Dearmer 1932: p. 443)

This is in contrast to the roughly contemporary Mackenzie, for whom 'Advent is a penitential season' (Mackenzie 1956: p. 232), linking his reasoning erroneously to the use of the colour purple, as if the liturgical colour determines the season rather than the other way around.

Liturgical scholarship firmly disagrees with this assumption, for example Cowley:

> The penitential frontal adorns the altar, it is true, and usually flowers are removed from the church, but little or nothing more suggests that this season is a penitential one.
>
> (Cowley 1960: p. 16)

The modern consensus is in favour of the joyful expectation referred to by Dearmer, and the concomitant theme of preparation. Thus for Elliott:

> The season with which the liturgical year begins is not penitential. Advent is a time of preparation and reflection, hope and anticipation.
>
> (Elliott 2002: p. 34)

Other recent Anglican commentators agree; Galley emphasizes that:

> . . . the season of preparation for Christmas . . . has a character very different from that of Lent . . . not a penitential season or a time of fasting. Essentially it is a time of joyful expectation, and it is this theme which predominates in the appointed lessons.
>
> (Galley 1989: p. 43)

Penitence is present in any case in the normal order of the Eucharist and implicitly as a part of what preparation entails. The cleansing of the thoughts of our hearts is referred to by the clearly (and historically) preparatory Collect for Purity. If preparation and joyful expectation are the dominant themes, however, the liturgy must above all reflect this. A note of joy is maintained in Advent partly by the continued use of 'Alleluia' in Gospel acclamations and elsewhere, whereas it is not to be said at all in Lent.

'Mood' is not something that can be 'switched on' or 'created' at will. Instead the aim should be for a quality of evocation rather than artificial contrivance, deliberately unfinished in order that it may resonate with and be taken up by individual worshippers and in their corporate celebration. The visual accent in Advent should be on dignified simplicity. Floral decoration is customarily not used. In earlier times use of the organ was severely restricted in Advent, as in Lent, but a looser interpretation would allow its dramatic capabilities to be used where appropriate, not least where the traditional Advent themes of Death, Judgement, Heaven and Hell are present, and in order to sound literal notes of joy in keeping with the season. From 17 December the imminent celebration of Christmas becomes the dominant theme, as reflected in the Advent Antiphons – the so-called 'Great Os' (see below).

Liturgical colours

The most common liturgical colour for Advent is now purple, but in parts of medieval England blue was the liturgical colour. Its revived use can usefully point to the distinctive character of Advent in relation to Lent. A darker shade of purple is often thought to be more in keeping with Advent than a lighter one to be associated with Lent. There is no precise rationale for these customs, but they can serve to mark the season effectively. David Kennedy suggests that in contrast to its use in Lent, in Advent 'the use of purple indicates more the sense that God's ultimate promises are awaiting fulfilment' (Kennedy 2006: p. 58). 'Rose pink' is an alternative on the Third Sunday of Advent (as it is on the Fourth Sunday of Lent, q.v.), originally because the Latin introit text for that day begins with the word *Gaudete*, 'rejoice', suggesting a more festive mood within the overall solemnity of the Advent season. Rose pink is still used in churches which possess vestments in this colour, although purchasing them for use on only two occasions in the year may not be felt to have priority when the purple of the rest of the season is a perfectly acceptable alternative. The possibility of rose colour should not be dismissed out of hand, however, as it forms part of the rich visual dimension of worship which can engage and instruct.

The Eucharist in Advent

TS does not provide a fully worked-out order for the Eucharist in Advent, but there are texts for use at the Eucharist during this season. In Advent, as in Lent, *Gloria in Excelsis* is not said or sung at the Eucharist, Sundays included because, as Kennedy remarks, 'it echoes the message of the angels to the shepherds [and] is held back until Christmas' (Kennedy 2006: p. 58). There are, however, two possible exceptions. The first is where St Andrew is celebrated according to its CW designation as a Festival; the second is the Eucharist for the Conception of the Blessed Virgin Mary (8 December) where this Lesser Festival in CW is kept locally as a Festival or Principal Feast. Even so, these occasions may not be observed on a Sunday in Advent, and so must be transferred to the nearest free weekday.

The Collect of the First Sunday of Advent has traditionally been repeated on the other three Sundays immediately after their proper collects. This sits uncomfortably with the liturgical understanding of the collect as a single prayer in this position, and so CW suggests its optional use as an unvarying post-Communion prayer on any day thereafter, including the Sundays. This option ought not to be taken up automatically, since individual prayers are provided for the subsequent Sundays and their following weekdays which make for sensible variety, and are in any case more suitable in terms of content for use in this way. The Advent Sunday collect could instead be used to conclude intercessions or might be printed as a private preparatory prayer in an Advent booklet.

The Roman Rite once enjoined the wearing of 'folded chasubles' by deacon and subdeacon at a High Mass (see Fortescue and O'Connell 1948: pp. 245–6, where the explanation of these is considerably longer than the general notes for the season), but modified this rule for smaller churches by directing alb, maniple and (for the deacon) stole, with no outer vestment. Consideration might be given to assisting ministers at a Solemn Eucharist or even any deacon at the Eucharist in Advent wearing alb and stole only, rather than with the dalmatic, in order to emphasize the simplicity of approach which the season invites. The same could apply to concelebrating priests, especially where the alternative is the wearing of matching white chasubles on account of the lack of sufficient purple ones.

The unity of the season should be borne in mind in the celebration of Lesser Festivals. For example, the proper collect may be said but the Advent readings prescribed for each day of the season could be continued; CW allows varying liturgical colours for Lesser Festivals in Advent but consideration could be given to vestments and hangings remaining in the colour of the season. A useful resource for those following the daily eucharistic lectionary and those who use the Roman Catholic Divine Office for daily prayer is Kevin W. Irwin, *Advent and Christmas: A Guide to the Eucharist and Hours* (Irwin

1986), which contains ample comment on the mood, imagery and scriptural texts for each day.

The Gathering and the Advent Wreath

In some churches it may be appropriate, if resources allow, to sing the Litany (BCP or CW) in procession on the Sundays of Advent as part of the Gathering. Alternatively, one of the longer Advent hymns may be sung. The president may wear a purple or blue cope for the procession, if changing to a chasuble before the greeting can be done unobtrusively, bearing in mind that to change vesture *can* erroneously imply that the liturgy proper begins after the procession. The Gathering might alternatively include the *asperges* (sprinkling) as part of the prayers of penitence. A suggested pattern for use where the Litany is sung is as follows:

- Litany in Procession.
- Silence.
- Confession.
- (*Kyrie*).
- Absolution.
- Hymn (altar censed; cope changed for chasuble).
- Greeting.
- Collect.

On Sundays, on arrival at the sanctuary consideration might be given to refraining from censing the altar on the grounds of emphasizing simplicity, even if incense will be used at the Gospel and Preparation of the Gifts, and during the Eucharistic Prayer. As an alternative in Advent, however, a fixed censer of bowl design standing near the altar could be used, incense being added by the president or a server at the beginning of the Gathering, at the Gospel, at the Intercessions, and at the beginning of the Eucharistic Prayer.

If the Litany is not used, the Gathering rite on Sundays might well feature use of the Advent Wreath with its candles, following the liturgical greeting and words of introduction. Traditionally there is a single white candle, representing the light of Christ coming into the world at Christmas (and therefore to be lit then), surrounded by three purple and one rose-pink candle, one for each Sunday of

Advent (the rose-pink candle for the third Sunday, *Gaudete*). Alternatively all the candles surrounding the central white one may be purple. TS gives texts for use at the lighting of each (pp. 51–5), in which children might be involved (see below for comment on the alternative texts). Alternatively, the Prayers of Penitence can supply the context for the use of the wreath, making use of *Kyrie* texts suggested in TS for each Sunday of the season (pp. 56–7) where this option is taken up. If this is done, the candle should be lit immediately before the Absolution, to associate the light with the forgiveness for which the assembly prays.

TS suggests further alternative places in the liturgy for the use of the wreath: after the Gospel, before the Peace or as the Prayer after Communion. Additional, dedicated material is provided as an alternative to the first set of texts. If one of these options is taken up, there is a risk that the strong visual character of the wreath will detract from the primary foci of Gospel, intercession and dismissal. David Kennedy sets out in detail the possibilities for using the Advent Wreath both within and outside the Eucharist (Kennedy 2006: pp. 65–72). In addition to the principal text (numbered 1) for each Sunday, the TS material (pp. 51–5, including a set of texts for Christmas Day) provides three more prayers for each occasion for use where children are present, including a text (number 3 in each case) for the congregation to say together which may follow the preceding text (number 2), intended for a single voice. There is no reason why the prayers associated with the Advent Wreath, wherever they are used in the service, may not be spoken by someone other than the president or other minister, especially in the case of the alternatives by a child or young adult.

Three alternative invitations to confession are given in TS (p. 34), all appropriate scriptural texts. While any could be used on any Sunday or weekday in Advent, the first would be particularly appropriate on the First Sunday and the second on the Second Sunday, as indicative of the overall feel of the season at its beginning and to associate the penitential rite with the collect and lectionary on the Third Sunday.

For the Prayers of Penitence TS gives three alternative *Kyrie* Confessions (pp. 34–5), the selection of which should be made in conjunction with the propers of the day, although none would be out of place at any time in the season. The availability of these texts should not automatically preclude the use of a corporate prayer of penitence. The lighting of the candles on the Advent Wreath can be incorporated into the Prayers of Penitence, forms for which are given in TS (see above).

The Liturgy of the Word

The Liturgy of the Word over the four Sundays of Advent might be the occasion for a sermon series, traditionally on the Four Last Things, but equally possibly on another quartet of themes which resonate with the liturgy of Advent and the disposition of the Church in the season, most obviously emphases suggested by the lectionary, respectively the Patriarchs, the Prophets, John the Baptist and the Blessed Virgin Mary. TS provides prayers for use with the Advent Wreath which reflect these. As an alternative to a gradual psalm on Sundays the Advent Prose, the *Rorate coeli*, could be used; one translation of this is provided in TS, and music is available in, for example, *The New English Hymnal* (hereafter NEH) at no. 501. An alternative is the less well-known Advent Sequence, *Salus aeterna*, again in NEH, no. 502. The *Rorate* has the advantage of having a repeated refrain conducive to confident congregational use.

Use of all three readings offered by the Sunday lectionary is preferable, with accompanying psalmody. A useful and succinct guide to the Sunday lectionary for Advent in all three years is given in Kennedy (2006: pp. 59–62). As a suggested Gospel acclamation, TS offers the text of Isaiah 40.3, reproduced from the CW main volume, and anticipates the Baptist's use of this prophecy. As such, it suggests the proclamation in the Gospel and the present reality of that which was long ago foretold. Further acclamations for Sunday and weekday use may be found in the *Weekday Missal* and, for Sundays, Young's *Enriching the Liturgy*; it is recommended that full use be made of these resources rather than having the same acclamation for the whole season.

Two forms of intercession are provided (TS: pp. 36–7), but should not be regarded as mandatory where local composition is possible, or alternative, imaginative and creative ways of offering the prayers of the people are appropriate. Incense may be added to a fixed censer (if used) at the beginning of the intercessions.

The Liturgy of the Sacrament

General issues concerning the Preparation of the Table are dealt with in detail in ALG 3 (pp. 57–65). Distinctive features for Advent could include the TS provision of three alternative Prayers at the Preparation of the Table (p. 38), and in order to mark this season (and other seasons) these could be used when such a prayer is not normally employed in Ordinary Time. The Roman Missal provides alternative prayers for Sunday and weekdays in Advent; these should be explored. Another very useful source is Alan Griffiths' *Celebrating the Christian Year*, vol. 3 (Griffiths 2005).

There is a rich provision in TS of eucharistic prefaces for Advent (pp. 39–40), some set to music in the *Common Worship: President's Edition* [hereafter PE], and full use should be made of these. As on any Sunday of the year the preface ought if possible to be sung, or at the very least the dialogue which precedes it. A proper preface for Advent should always be used with Prayers A, B, C (C admits a short preface only) and E. Prayers D, F and G are fixed texts, but F refers to 'the signs of your kingdom' and 'the coming of your Son Jesus Christ', allusions to Advent themes, so might well be used on some occasions. Of the short prefaces provided by TS, the first associates themes of redemption and judgement with the nativity, which suggest its appropriate use in the fourth week of Advent. The third option recalls the role of John the Baptist and is therefore especially appropriate on the Third Sunday of Advent since it ties in with the collect of that day. The immediacy of the language of the final short preface suggests its use in the final days before Christmas, perhaps from *O Sapientia* (17 December) onwards. On weekdays careful selection should be made in conjunction with the lectionary and the intercessions.

The first extended preface in TS, to be used with Prayer A, B, C or E, is specifically for use from the First Sunday of Advent until 18 December. The second extended preface is for use from 17 December (*O Sapientia*) until Christmas Eve. Appropriately for the final days of Advent and conscious of the imagery and scriptural provision of the foregoing weeks, the roles of the prophets, the Blessed Virgin and John the Baptist are drawn into a single narrative. Music for both extended prefaces is found in PE.

The Dismissal

TS offers two simple and two solemn blessings for use in Advent (p. 41). Use of the solemn blessings (sung if possible) is to be preferred on Sundays, but is not appropriate for weekdays, when a simple blessing should always be used, but not omitted in favour of the dismissal only (for a discussion of this matter in general, see ALG 3, pp. 77–8).

Advent provides an opportunity to use the form of Alternative Dismissal in TS (pp. 42–3). This clearly has the older tradition of the 'Last Gospel' in mind, and could be used on Sundays (only) to balance liturgically the use of the Advent Wreath as part of the Gathering in the overall cause of marking the distinctiveness of the season, or at least the beginning of it on Advent Sunday. The Gospel passage included is brief enough so as not to detract from the liturgical Gospel earlier in the rite, although it might still be felt that it 'repeats' the liturgical emphasis on the proclamation of the Gospel in the Liturgy of the Word. The blessing and dismissal are integral to the alternative form, the dismissal texts slightly lengthened to give seasonal flavour.

Processions, antiphons and Advent Carol Services

The season offers opportunities for exploring its themes in ways additional to the regular celebration of the Eucharist. An 'Advent Procession' in the form of a sequence of prayer, music and readings for the season can be an effective way to conclude Advent Sunday in the evening. For this and for Advent Carol Services material is provided in TS (pp. 44–9), although many places follow local custom on these occasions. They key is to strike a balance between the visual, the auditory and the participatory, to give a sense of the Church in pilgrimage towards the joy of the Lord's appearing. A procession should ideally include the whole congregation, not just the clergy, choir and servers, although large numbers and limited space may not make this practicable. If the church has copes of subdued colours (especially purple and blue, but never black) processions in Advent would be good opportunities in which to use them.

The possibilities for liturgies of this type are many, and there now exist many resources on which to draw, some of which are included in TS. This is an opportunity for principled local creativity: a planning group might be given responsibility for such a service, although the parish priest, while acting as an adviser and guide, should have the final word in the capacity of liturgical president of the community.

Advent Carol Services

The TS material begins with three examples of Bidding Prayers and Introductions (pp. 44–5) all of which richly evoke the liturgical character of Advent without pre-empting Christmas. The third concludes with a period of silent prayer and the Collect of Advent Sunday.

TS provides four alternative patterns of readings (pp. 46–7), each offering six scripture readings with associated psalmody, a canticle and a Gospel reading. The themes of each pattern explore the meaning and implications of the season to good effect: that entitled 'The King and his kingdom' might be used nearer the beginning of Advent to emphasize the transition from the 'kingship of Christ' focus of the weeks immediately preceding it, although an alternative Gospel for use 'at Christmas' is also provided. The canticles are cross-referenced to *Common Worship: Daily Prayer* (hereafter DP), a useful reminder that the Daily Office plays a crucial part in the celebration of this season and itself offers many opportunities (see Chapter 7 of this book). Clergy and communities should not feel bound to the exact letter of these patterns – others may suggest themselves, and local adaptations may always be made, for example on the grounds of the likely total length of a service once music is added. The TS material offers six suggested 'Conclusions', all responsorial in character, with the suggestion of one of the blessings or the ending given in the seasonal material (p. 41). At an Advent Service on Advent Sunday it might even be appropriate to use the Alternative Dismissal given on pp. 42–3 where this has not been used at the principal Eucharist. In the days immediately before Christmas, as suggested in TS pp. 58–9, the 'Great O' antiphons might be used as the framework for an extended liturgical meditation.

3

Christmas

And now we give you thanks
because, in the incarnation of the Word,
a new light has dawned upon the world;
you have become one with us
that we might become one with you in your glorious kingdom.
(Short Preface for Christmas, TS: p. 72)

Liturgical character

The tradition of there being '12 days of Christmas', from Christmas Day to the Epiphany has, in the Church of England at least, given way to an extended 40-day celebration of the incarnation from Christmas Day to Candlemas, parallel to the 50 days of Easter. As TS makes clear, Christmas is much more than the celebration of Jesus' birthday (p. 64) but, for various reasons, the proclamation of the truth of the Word becoming flesh for us and for our salvation can easily get squeezed out of a 12-day holiday period. This 40-day observance, first suggested by the Liturgical Commission in PHG and incorporated into the CW calendar seven years later, in 1998, allows the incarnation and its significance for the life and mission of the Church to be explored in greater depth than was possible during the 12 days, before Ordinary Time begins. That said, the 12 days still have a distinctive character of their own which should be observed as fully as possible, even when, because this festival is anticipated for such a long period, it is tempting to give up on Christmas as soon as the day itself has passed.

Liturgically speaking, the celebration of Christmas begins at Evening Prayer on Christmas Eve, except that the Collect of Christmas Eve is used at that service and a Christmas Collect is not used until the first Eucharist of Christmas. Unlike the Easter octave, which precludes the celebration of any Principal Feast or Festival falling within it, Christmas Day is followed by three distinctive festivals: Stephen, the first martyr; John the Evangelist; and the Holy Innocents (for texts, see CF, pp. 119–32). If one of these falls on the Sunday after Christmas, CW, unlike the ASB, permits it to be observed on that Sunday, thus giving these Christmas festivals greater prominence than they have had hitherto.

Apart from the feasts of Stephen and the Holy Innocents when red is used, gold or white is the liturgical colour for the Christmas season. Where a church possesses gold vestments, it would be appropriate to wear them, rather than white, until Epiphany, to distinguish the 12 days from the weeks which follow. At the Eucharist, the *Gloria in Excelsis* is used daily from Christmas Day until the festival of the Naming and Circumcision of Jesus (1 January) and again on Epiphany. The Creed is only said on Christmas Day and on the Epiphany.

The Lesser Festival of the martyr Thomas Becket falls on 29 December. Unless he has a particular local significance, it would be appropriate to use the readings for the fifth day of Christmas at a Eucharist on this day (unless, of course, it is the First Sunday of Christmas), with the Collect of Christmas Day, and to observe Thomas Becket as a Commemoration, mentioning him in the Prayers of Intercession.

The crib provides the principal symbolic focus for devotion at Christmas. Although its location within the church will depend partly on the shape and layout of the building, Elliott is surely right to discourage it being placed under or in front of the altar (Elliott 2002: p. 41). Whether it remains in place until Epiphany (when the Magi appear and the crib is transformed into an 'Epiphany House') or Candlemas, the crib merits its own space so that members of the assembly can have easy access to it, not least before and after services. It is appropriate for worshippers and visitors to be encouraged to light candles in front of the crib, and for prayer cards to be made available. The prayers at the crib (TS: pp. 103–4) are particularly suitable for this purpose. One of these prayers may also be used if a station is made at the crib during the entrance procession on Christmas morning and on the First and, when there is one, Second Sundays of Christmas. The entrance hymn could be broken so that the prayer can be said and, if incense is used, the crib censed with three double swings before the hymn resumes.

Eucharist of Christmas Night or Morning

TS provides a fully worked-out order for the principal celebration of the Eucharist at Christmas (pp. 77–87). In most communities this will be the Midnight Mass. However, in churches where, for pastoral or practical reasons, Midnight Mass is not celebrated, it may be used on Christmas morning or, indeed, at an earlier point on Christmas Eve. In those parishes, perhaps the majority, where there will be more than one Christmas Eucharist, this rite would normally be used at Midnight Mass, with material from the general section for the Christmas season (pp. 65–76) enriching the other celebrations.

Until relatively recently, most parishes could assume that the Midnight Mass would attract the largest congregation of all the Christmas services, if not of the whole year, with the parish's Sunday congregation being joined by a significant number of occasional worshippers and visitors, many of whom would be communicants. Such popularity would undoubtedly have been disapproved of by Percy Dearmer, whose experience of this service, at the end of the nineteenth century, led him 'to doubt whether the revival of the Midnight Mass is desirable under modern conditions of life' (Dearmer 1932: p. 446).

In the relatively recent past, different 'conditions of life' have led, in many places, to an all-age non-eucharistic celebration on Christmas Eve, whether a Crib Service or a Christingle, attracting significantly greater numbers than Midnight Mass. Such services seem to meet the needs of those who want to go to church at Christmas in a way that, for a century, Midnight Mass did. That said, in many parishes and cathedrals Midnight Mass congregations are by no means small, but compared with the past will often contain a higher percentage of those who are not regular members of the worshipping community; in fact, in some places they will outnumber them. Such trends are by no means universal and will depend on a number of factors, not least geographical and demographic. While they cannot be discussed in any greater detail here, they do highlight the need for local communities to consider the make-up of their congregation at Midnight Mass, for its composition will undoubtedly affect the way in which the rite is celebrated.

Gold or white is the liturgical colour for this celebration. The church's best vestments should be worn and, in churches where incense is used only occasionally, it is particularly appropriate on this feast. The president should wear a chasuble throughout the rite unless a cope is worn for the blessing of the crib (see below). If the president is assisted by one or more priests, this is a particularly appropriate occasion for concelebration (for a discussion of concelebration, see ALG 3, pp. 15–18) and, if no deacon is present, they may read the Gospel, prepare the altar, supervise the ablutions and, where it is used, proclaim the dismissal Gospel.

To symbolize the fact that, in Christ, 'a new light has dawned upon the world' (TS: p. 72), it is appropriate for hand-held candles to be given to the congregation as they arrive and for them to be lit before the service starts. They may remain lit until the end of the Gospel and, if the Johannine prologue is read at the Dismissal, lit again for that. After the liturgy, some members of the congregation may like to leave them in front of the crib or before an image of the Blessed Virgin Mary.

In addition to lections for a second and third service, CW provides three principal sets of readings for Christmas Night and/or Christmas Day, from which Set III, which corresponds with the BCP provision, must be used at one of the principal celebrations (MV: p. 544). In the Roman tradition, readings are provided for a Vigil Mass (which is not the Mass of Christmas Eve, but the first Mass of Christmas, which may be celebrated during the afternoon of 24 December, before or after the first Evening Prayer of Christmas), a Midnight Mass, a Mass of the Dawn and a Mass of the Day. Comparing these with the CW provision, Table 3 suggests one way in which the latter may be used.

Blessing of the Crib

In some churches the crib is blessed before Midnight Mass, often at an all-age service where a large number of children are present. Where this is the case, Elliott suggests that the blessing may be repeated at the midnight celebration (Elliott 2002: p. 40), and that seems particularly appropriate if a significant proportion of the midnight congregation were not present at the earlier service.

There are three possible positions for the blessing of the crib at the Midnight Mass: before the Gathering, within the Gathering, and at the Dismissal. Elliott assumes that the blessing of the crib is not

Table 3 Comparison of RC and CW readings for Christmas

RC		*CW*	
Vigil Mass	Isaiah 62.1–5 Psalm 89.2–4, 15–16, 26, 28 Acts 13.16–17, 22–25 Matthew 1.[1–17] 18–end	3rd Service	Isaiah 62.1–5 Psalms 110, 117 Matthew 1.18–end
Midnight Mass	Isaiah 9.1–7 Psalm 96.1–3, 11–13 Titus 2.11–14 Luke 2.1–14	Set I	Isaiah 9.2–7 Psalm 96 Titus 2.11–14 Luke 2.1–14 [15–20]
Mass of the Dawn	Isaiah 62.11–end Psalm 97.1, 6, 11–12 Titus 3.4–7 Luke 2.15–20	Set II	Isaiah 62.6–12 Psalm 97 Titus 3.4–7 Luke 2.[1–7] 8–20
Mass of the Day	Isaiah 52.7–10 Psalm 98.1–7 Hebrews 1.1–6 John 1.1–5 [6–8] 9–14 [15–18]	Set III	Isaiah 52.7–10 Psalm 98 Hebrews 1.1–4 [5–12] John 1.1–14

part of the Mass proper, and therefore directs that the priest, wearing eucharistic vestments or a cope, should carry the bambino (the image of the infant Christ) on a cushion to the crib before the entrance hymn is sung. The crib is blessed, and then the procession moves to the altar, the cope, if worn, being changed for a chasuble after the altar has been censed (Elliott 2002: p. 40).

TS also suggests that the crib should be blessed at the beginning of the service, but as part of the Gathering (p. 77). In this position, a change from cope to chasuble is less appropriate. A carol may be sung as the procession moves to the crib. 'Once in Royal David's City', famously used at the beginning of the King's College Service of Nine Lessons and Carols, works well in this position, whether or not it is possible for the first verse to be sung as a solo. If the prayers of penitence do not take place at the crib, the hymn could be split in half so that the first part is sung as the procession moves to the crib, and the second part as it moves to the sanctuary or place where the Liturgy of the Word is celebrated. Even if the Prayers of Penitence do take place at the crib, the last verse of the hymn could be sung after the Prayer of Blessing, while the crib is being sprinkled with water and censed.

There is also a tradition of the crib being blessed at the end of the Mass. *Ritual Notes* refers to this (edition of 1946 [1894], p. 313), as does Geoffrey Wright (Wright 1994: pp. 8–9). When this practice is adopted, the president, wearing a chasuble, carries the bambino in the entrance procession and places it in the centre of the altar. It can be censed with three double swings when the altar is censed, but should be moved to one side of the altar, or to another table, from the offertory to the end of the ablutions. If 'O Come, All Ye Faithful' is used as the entrance hymn, it could conclude with the penultimate verse, 'Sing, choirs of angels', the final verse, 'Yea, Lord, we greet thee', being kept back until after the blessing of the crib, when it could be sung immediately before the final dismissal, as described below.

The Gathering

Gathering at the crib at the beginning of the rite, TS provides optional opening words from *In the Holy Nativity of Our Lord* by Richard Crashaw (*c.* 1613–49) with an alternative responsive form from David Silk's *Prayers for Use at the Alternative Services* (1986). Given the generally accepted convention that no words should be spoken by the president before greeting the people, either of these texts, if used, should be spoken by someone other than the president. Indeed, they could be read more effectively from the lectern or pulpit at the beginning of the liturgy, before the procession to the crib. At whichever point they are used, there is a danger that some of those present, particularly visitors, may consider themselves to be welcomed as 'all wonders in one sight', in which case it may be more appropriate to omit them altogether!

Although TS does not preface the greeting with the Trinitarian invocation, it may, of course, be used, particularly if it is the normal practice of the community to begin the Eucharist in this way.

At the blessing of the crib, it would make sense for the president to face the people to say the words of introduction, and then turn to the crib to bless it. The bambino may be placed inside the crib either as soon as the procession arrives there or after the words of introduction have been said. If there are children present, they may be encouraged to gather round. At the appropriate point in the prayer, the president blesses the crib with the sign of the cross. The crib may then be sprinkled with holy water and incensed.

The Prayers of Penitence, whether used at the crib or later in the service, can be led by a minister other than the president. If these take place at the crib, the procession moves to the sanctuary during the *Gloria in Excelsis* which, although optional in TS, should always be used at Midnight Mass, the congregation echoing the song of the angels. The ministers reverence and kiss the altar in the usual way and, if incense is used, the altar is censed before the president moves to the chair for the collect. If there is no choir to lead the singing of the *Gloria*, or a significant proportion of the congregation are not regular worshippers, a metrical version of the canticle or, even 'Angels from the Realms of Glory' could be sung.

If the Prayers of Penitence do not take place at the crib, the procession moves to the sanctuary after the crib has been blessed, either during the second half of the entrance hymn or while another hymn is sung. The ministers reverence and kiss the altar (the altar is censed), and the Prayers of Penitence follow, unless it is local custom for them to follow the Prayers of Intercession. The Gathering concludes with the collect, the president using the appropriate prayer, either for Midnight Mass or for a Eucharist celebrated on Christmas Day.

The Liturgy of the Word

The Liturgy of the Word continues in the usual way. For the Gospel acclamation, the triple alleluia, when sung, may, as Kennedy suggests, 'diminish participation when there are many visitors' (Kennedy 2006: p. 86). Although it could be proclaimed loudly before and after the Gospel, if the Set I readings are used with the shortened form of the Lukan birth narrative, 'While Shepherds Watched' is an appropriate hymn to herald it, the last verse being sung at the end of the reading, with the final Gospel response omitted. Thus:

Gospeller And suddenly there was with the angels a multitude of the heavenly host, praising God and saying:

All **All glory be to God on high**
And on the earth be peace;
Good-will, henceforth from heaven to men
Begin and never cease.

Depending on its position in the church, it may be appropriate to read the Gospel from the crib. If Set III is used and John 1.1–14 is read, although Kennedy suggests that it is the custom 'in more catholic traditions' to bow or genuflect at 'And the Word was made flesh and dwelt among us', this is no longer required (Kennedy 2006: p. 86).

An authorized translation of the Nicene Creed must be used at every celebration of the Eucharist on this Principal Feast. In the Roman tradition it is customary for the whole assembly to genuflect at the *et incarnatus est*, 'was incarnate from the Holy Spirit and the Virgin Mary and was made man' (GIRM: p. 137), as is also the case on the Feast of the Annunciation.

The Liturgy of the Sacrament

Although the Liturgy of the Sacrament in this rite contains no distinctive features, if a significant number of those present are not regular worshippers, some accommodations to the community's normal pattern of worship may be appropriate. For example, a responsorial or metrical form of the *Sanctus*, *Benedictus* and *Agnus Dei* may be more effective than a congregational setting; and a meditative carol, such as 'Silent Night', could be sung during the breaking of the bread. Equally, in places where the modern language version of the Lord's Prayer is most commonly used, the modified traditional form may be more appropriate on this occasion.

If there are likely to be a large number of communicants, consideration needs to be given to how many vessels are used, when they are placed on the altar, and whether it is possible to transfer the consecrated elements from a large ciborium or dish and flagon to smaller vessels at the time of distribution, so as to prevent the altar from appearing cluttered during the Eucharistic Prayer. For a more detailed discussion of this, see ALG 3, pp. 25–6. To assist with the administration of the sacrament, Communion stations placed around the church may usefully supplement the normal method of distribution.

The Dismissal

TS provides for John 1.1–14, the so-called last Gospel from the medieval Mass, to be proclaimed as a dismissal Gospel either before or after the Blessing. If this is to happen, readings from Set I or Set II must be used for the Liturgy of the Word. Since, in most people's minds, the Blessing is so clearly associated with the end of a service, there is a danger that the dismissal Gospel will lose its impact if the Blessing has preceded it. Whenever this option is used, consideration needs to be given as to where it should be proclaimed from. One possibility would be to read it at the crib where, as has already been suggested, it could form part of a concluding rite which includes the blessing of the crib. Even in churches where it is not customary for the Gospel to be sung, to emphasize the centrality of this passage on this feast, a sung Gospel would be appropriate.

If the crib is to be blessed as part of the Dismissal, the following is an example of the way in which this might be done. Following the prayer after Communion, a procession is formed and, led by the thurifer, moves to the crib, the president carrying the bambino. Although the president may wear a cope for this procession, the practice of also wearing a humeral veil, referred to by Wright (Wright 1994: p. 9), does not seem appropriate, as this confuses the image of the Christ-child, which is a focus for devotion during the Christmas season, with the Blessed Sacrament, in which Christ, crucified, risen and ascended, may be adored. A Christmas hymn, such as 'Hark, the Herald Angels Sing', accompanies the procession, during which hand-held candles are relit and some of the congregation, particularly any children, might be encouraged to gather round or at least face the crib. At the end of the hymn, while the president continues to hold the bambino, the Johannine prologue is proclaimed by a deacon or other minister, the Gospel Book being censed as at the Liturgy of the Word. At the words, 'And the Word was made flesh and dwelt among us', the bambino is put into the crib which, at the end of the Gospel, is blessed as described above. As the crib is being sprinkled with holy water and censed, a carol, such as 'Away in a Manger', may be sung. If both the dismissal Gospel and the blessing of the crib take place at the Dismissal, one of the shorter Christmas blessings, rather than the 'solemn' form provided in TS, may appropriately be used, to prevent the concluding rite from becoming too wordy. After the final Blessing, the verse beginning 'Yea, Lord, we greet thee' is sung, the ministers kneeling before the crib at the words 'O come, let us adore him'. The rite concludes with the Dismissal.

Where the dismissal Gospel and blessing of the crib are not combined, a procession to the crib could still be made and 'Yea, Lord, we greet thee' sung as a response to the Gospel, before the president gives the final blessing.

Christmas Carol Services

Christmas Carol Services can vary enormously in terms of their structure and content, decisions about both of which will be governed by a number of factors, not least the location of the service, when it is to be celebrated, the nature of the congregation and the musical resources available. While many groups and organizations, from primary schools to City law firms, now hold Christmas Carol Services in churches, chapels and cathedrals, clergy and lay worship leaders often find themselves leading, or taking part in, Carol Services in 'secular' locations as diverse as residential homes for the elderly or local supermarkets.

Although such a variety of circumstances will require very different treatments, basic advice is to ensure that if a liturgical celebration is intended (in other words, if it is not purely 'carol singing'), it should have a definite liturgical structure and contain properly liturgical material. This should normally include a sequence of scripture readings and an opportunity for intercessory prayer, which may take the form of a bidding prayer. TS provides resources for these (pp. 88–91), including the traditional King's College, Cambridge bidding prayer and pattern of readings devised by the Dean, Eric Milner-White, for their first Service of Nine Lessons and Carols in 1918. Where this is used, the broad scope of the bidding prayer will often make further intercession unnecessary. In many situations, nine readings are felt to be too many, and so the number is reduced. Because it is referred to in the bidding prayer, the account of the Fall should normally be read as the first lesson, and the Johannine prologue conclude the sequence. After the ninth lesson, Milner-White's order concludes with the Collect of Christmas Eve and a final blessing (TS: p. 73, P *1*).

TS provides two other bidding prayers: one adapted from a text by David Silk, and a new composition. If the latter is used, which is more of an introduction to the service than a series of biddings, intercessory material, such as TS, pp. 67–71, should be included later in the service.

TS also provides two sequences of readings in addition to the King's College pattern: 'Good news for the poor', which contains five readings from the prophets, followed by St Paul's servant song (Philippians 2.5–11) and concludes with the Lukan birth narrative, if used at Christmas, or the Annunciation to Mary, if the service takes place in Advent; and 'The Gospel of Luke' which, specifically intended for use in Christmastide, contains passages from the first two chapters of Luke's Gospel, from the Annunciation to Zechariah to the Presentation in the Temple, and concludes with verses from Titus chapters 2 and 3, which proclaims the truth that the grace of God has appeared for the salvation of all.

It is very common for Christmas Carol Services to take place before Christmas, and, given the pastoral and evangelistic opportunities provided by such celebrations, there are now very few purists who would prohibit this. In CCW1 it was remarked that:

> For example, school and university terms end . . . well before 25 December, and it would seem churlish to deny those closely defined communities the chance to celebrate Christ's birth before they depart for the vacation. This makes the point that mission and Christian celebration are geared towards communities as well as individuals, and use of the Calendar in mission must always acknowledge this, even if it means departing from the strict letter. There is a place for the imagination, and a necessity to recall that no amount of order and structure on the part of human beings can confine the God who reaches out to us in love and compassion.
>
> (CCW1: 2001, p. 49)

If communities are able to celebrate separate Advent and Christmas Carol Services, even if the latter falls in Advent, then while trying to include a sense of expectant anticipation of the coming feast, the Christmas service can focus primarily on the incarnation. If only one Carol Service is celebrated before Christmas then, while legitimately incorporating Christmas material, consideration should be given to also including at least some recognition of Advent, taking advantage of its powerful themes of preparation and expectation, as described in Chapter 2.

Gold or white is the liturgical colour for a Christmas Carol Service, and in some circumstances the officiant may wear a white cope (over a cotta or surplice), even if the service takes place in Advent. If the crib has already been erected, a procession to the crib, either for the proclamation of the final reading, or for prayers of intercession, might be appropriate. Incense could be used for the procession and, if the final reading comes from one of the Gospels, the Gospel Book could be censed, as at the Eucharist. Depending on the layout of the church, children could be invited to gather around the crib, and the congregation light hand-held candles, which they could take away with them or leave burning in stands or buckets of sand in front of the crib.

In churches where eucharistic devotions and Benediction of the Blessed Sacrament form part of the regular pattern of worship (for a discussion of Benediction, see the notes on Corpus Christi in ALG 6), the sacrament may be exposed after the final reading, and intercessions may be offered before it. In place of the *Tantum Ergo*, verses from 'O Come, All Ye Faithful', with its refrain, 'O come, let us adore him', may be sung. The service may conclude with Benediction.

Christingle and Crib Services

Popular either before or after Christmas, in many communities the Christingle Service has become one of the best attended services of the year. Based on a Moravian custom, and now widely used in the Church of England and other denominations, it raises awareness of, and funds for, the work of the Children's Society with a highly visual and participatory act of worship which is especially accessible to children and families. The 'Christingle' ('Christ light'), which is sometimes made as part of the service, usually consists of an orange (representing the world), with a red ribbon tied around it (representing Christ's blood shed on the cross), decorated with sweets (representing the fruits of the earth), sometimes skewered on four cocktail sticks (representing the four seasons), with a candle pushed into the centre of the orange (symbolizing Christ the light of the world).

TS provides an outline for a Christingle Service together with some textual resources for use at different points in the service (pp. 92, 94–101). In PHG the meaning of the service is discussed in detail, and there are also a number of practical suggestions. The Children's Society's website (<www.childrenssociety.org.uk>) also provides a number of useful visual and electronic resources. Even if a church doesn't usually use a data projector, it may be particularly useful at a Christingle Service attended by a large number of people, when the making and symbolism of the Christingle can be explained by the use of images projected on to a screen or wall. Alternatively, foam or another suitable material can be used to make a giant Christingle!

A Crib Service is likely to be held in church on Christmas Eve or the Fourth Sunday of Advent, and may also form the basis of a final act of worship for infant and primary school children before the Christmas holiday. The same resource material provided for a Christingle Service may also be used at a Crib Service, for which TS also gives an outline order (p. 93), in which the central element is the building of the crib, which presents the opportunity to tell the Christmas story. As with the Christingle Service, this service works best when it involves the active participation of a number of the children present. Those who are able to practise beforehand can assist with readings and leading the prayers. Others can take part in the building of the crib and, when it is complete, gather round with hand-held candles while prayers are offered. If the bambino is not placed in the crib until Midnight Mass, children may be encouraged to return during the Christmas season to see it in place. In some church schools, and in churches where there are a significant number of communicant children, the building of the crib can form the Liturgy of the Word within a short, simple celebration of the Eucharist.

New Year

New Year's Day is celebrated in the Church of England as the festival of the Naming and Circumcision of Jesus, a title which combines BCP and ASB titles of this feast. In many churches it is customary for a Eucharist to be celebrated on this day, for which CF provides suitable resources (pp. 37–41). The *Gloria in Excelsis* should be used, and the hymn, 'How Sweet the Name of Jesus Sounds', upon which the intercessions for this day in CF are based, is particularly appropriate.

In some communities, a 'Watch Night' service, beginning late on 31 December and continuing past midnight, marks the arrival of the New Year. Such a celebration provides an opportunity for reflection on, and thanksgiving for, the past year, and prayer for God's blessing on the new one. This Moravian custom was adopted by Charles Wesley, and has a special place within the Reformed tradition. Some of the resource material in TS may be suitable for such a celebration (pp. 105–15) and PHG suggests that a Vigil Service, beginning with the Blessing of Light, would also be appropriate (PHG: p. 200). It is customary in some churches for Benediction of the Blessed Sacrament to be given at midnight, and this may conclude any form of 'Watch Night' celebration.

This section in TS also contains material from the Methodist Covenant Service. Drawn from *The Methodist Worship Book* (1999), it provides an opportunity for God's people to renew their covenant relationship with him within the context of the Eucharist. When used, the covenant is renewed (TS: pp. 108–12) in response to the proclamation of God's word, and would therefore most naturally follow the sermon, the creed being omitted. Since the act of renewal is prefaced by a substantial penitential section, it would be appropriate to omit the prayers of penitence during the Gathering. Regrettably, TS has omitted Wesley's hymn, 'Come, Let Us Use the Grace Divine', which acts as a bridge between the penitential rite and the renewal of the covenant. Wesley's words are most commonly sung to *Kingsfold*, the Vaughan Williams arrangement of an English folk song, the second half of the tune being used for the last verse:

Come, let us use the grace divine,
And all, with one accord,
In a perpetual cov'nant join
Ourselves to Christ the Lord.
Give up ourselves through Jesu's power,
His name to glorify;
And promise, to this sacred hour,
For God to live and die.

The cov'nant we this moment make
Be ever kept in mind:
We will no more our God forsake,
Or cast his words behind.
We never will throw off his fear
Who hears our solemn vow;
And if thou art well pleased to hear,
Come down, and meet us now.

To each the cov'nant blood apply,
Which takes our sins away;
And register our names on high,
And keep us to that day.
(*The Methodist Worship Book*,
1999: p. 287)

After the community has renewed the covenant, the rite continues with some brief, responsive intercessions and a concluding prayer, which leads naturally into the Peace.

4

Epiphany

And now we give you thanks
because, in the wonder of the incarnation,
your eternal Word has brought to the eyes of faith
a new and radiant vision of your glory.
In him we see our God made visible
and so are caught up in love of the God we cannot see.
(Short Preface for Epiphany, TS: p. 131)

Liturgical character

The Western Church's celebration of the Epiphany on 6 January has concentrated almost exclusively on the visit of the Magi. In the Eastern tradition, from at least the fourth century, three epiphanies or manifestations of the incarnate God have been associated with this date, three different ways in which the 'eternal Word has brought to the eyes of faith a new and radiant vision' of God's glory: the visit of the Magi, the Baptism of Christ, and the turning of water into wine at the wedding in Cana.

That there should be an Epiphany season (hence, in CW, Sundays *of* rather than *after* Epiphany), combined with the 12 days of Christmas to provide a 40-day celebration of the incarnation from Christmas to Candlemas, parallel to the 50 days of Easter, has already been discussed at the beginning of the previous chapter. While some may still prefer to follow the BCP or Roman Catholic pattern of beginning Ordinary Time on the day after the Epiphany (BCP) or the day following the feast of the Baptism of Christ (Roman Catholic), there is a great deal of sense in the CW scheme of a combined season of Christmas and Epiphany which does away with awkward, brief returns to 'green' days that adherence to the strict letter of traditional Western observance entails. On the other hand, such an elision of themes might be thought somewhat contrived, in the way that the wholly novel 'Kingdom' season between All Saints and Advent (q.v.), introduced in PHG, was so regarded by some; yet ironically CW itself can produce such a brief period when Candlemas falls near the beginning of Lent. Also to be remembered, however, is that characteristic of liturgical time which is not wholly under our organizing control, and which speaks of the unpredictable activity of God (see Chapter 1 of this book).

If Epiphany is combined with Christmas to provide a 40-day celebration of the incarnation, white should be used as the liturgical colour until the Presentation. The season begins with Evening Prayer on the eve of the Epiphany and concludes with the last service on the Feast of the Presentation (whether it is celebrated on 2 February or transferred to the nearest Sunday). At the Eucharist, the *Gloria in Excelsis* is only required to be said on Sundays and on the feasts of the Epiphany, the Conversion of Paul (for which full provision can be found in CF, pp. 42–6) and the Presentation; the same is true for the Creed, except that it need not be said on the festival of the Conversion of Paul.

Eucharistic and non-eucharistic services during this season may be enriched by the material provided in TS (pp. 121–37). There is also extensive provision connected with the theme of unity which may be used during the Week of Prayer for Christian Unity (18–25 January). The Alternative Dismissal (p. 146) would be particularly appropriate on the Sunday which falls within the octave. Celebration of the manifestation of God's glory also encourages prayer for the mission of the Church and, again, TS provides suitable resources which may be used on weekdays and Sundays (pp. 149–58).

Although they do not appear in TS, there are two further customs associated with the Feast of the Epiphany: the blessing of chalk and the solemn proclamation of the date of Easter. Each of these will be described briefly here. In considering whether either or both should be used, care must be taken that the liturgy of the day is not overloaded, particularly if the TS order is followed, with its presentation of the Epiphany gifts and dismissal Gospel.

Particularly in central Europe, it is common for chalk to be blessed and distributed on the Feast of the Epiphany, so that it may be used to mark the names of the Magi as well as the year on the doorpost or lintel of the houses of Christians. This symbolizes prayer for Christ's blessing on the homes of his people as well as the

Christian's willingness to offer hospitality to the Magi on their journey and, by extension, to welcome all visitors in the name of Christ. Wright suggests that the chalk should be blessed after the Gospel, but it could also take place at another suitable point in the rite, perhaps informally during the notices. The chalk is placed on a tray and the following form may be used, or adapted:

President + Our help is in the name of the Lord,
All **who has made heaven and earth.**

President The Lord be with you
All **and also with you.**

President Lord God, among the gifts of your creation you have given chalk to be of benefit to us all. We call on your holy name to bless + these pieces of chalk. May those who take them and write with them on the doors of their houses the names of your holy Wise Men, Kaspar, Melchior and Balthasar, be aided by their intercession and have a share in their merits; may their bodies be healthy and their souls saved. We ask this through Christ our Lord.
All **Amen.**

The chalk is then sprinkled with holy water and may be distributed at the end of the Eucharist. In the year 2009, the door of the house may be marked as follows:

20 + K + M + B + 09

Wright suggests the following prayer which may be said as the door is marked:

The three wise men:

K Kaspar
M Melchior
B and Balthasar

followed the star of God's Son who became man:

20 two thousand
09 and nine years ago.
++ May Christ bless our home
++ and remain with us through the year.
(Wright 1994: pp. 9–10, 38–9)

The solemn proclamation of the date of Easter, and of other festivals whose dates are dependent upon it, dates back to a time when there were no personal calendars and diaries. Nowadays, such a proclamation has the value of emphasizing the centrality of Easter; in Elliott's words, 'to remind us that the whole liturgical year takes its meaning from the risen Saviour' (Elliott 2002: p. 43). The proclamation is traditionally made by a deacon but, in the absence of a deacon, may be made by another minister or cantor. According to Elliott, it may take place after the Gospel, the sermon or the Prayer after Communion, and should be made from the lectern, pulpit or another prominent place. Wherever possible it should be sung to a simple chant. Wright provides an example of a pointed text (Wright 1994: p. 40). The following version, from the Roman Catholic Church, could be used, or adapted for use, in an Anglican context:

Dear brothers and sisters, the glory of the Lord has shone upon us,
and shall ever be manifest among us, until the day of his return.
Through the rhythms of times and seasons
let us celebrate the mysteries of salvation.

Let us recall the year's culmination, the Easter Triduum of the Lord:
his last supper, his crucifixion, his burial and his rising
celebrated between the evening of the *date* of *month* [*Maundy Thursday*]
and the evening of the *date* of *month* [*Easter Sunday*].

Each Easter – as on each Sunday –
the Holy Church makes present the great and saving deed
by which Christ has for ever conquered sin and death.

From Easter are reckoned all the days we keep holy.
Ash Wednesday, the beginning of Lent, will occur on the *date* of *month*.

The Ascension of the Lord will be commemorated on the *date* of *month.*
Pentecost, the joyful conclusion of the season of Easter,
will be celebrated on the *date* of *month.*
And this year the First Sunday of Advent will be on the *date* of *month.*

Likewise the pilgrim Church proclaims the passover of Christ
in the feasts of the holy Mother of God,
in the feasts of the Apostles and Saints,
and in the commemoration of the faithful departed.

To Jesus Christ, who was, who is, and who is to come,
Lord of time and history,
be endless praise, for ever and ever.
Amen. (Amen. Amen.)

(Elliott 2002: pp. 204–5)

The Eucharist on the Feast of the Epiphany

The Feast of the Epiphany, when anchored immovably to 6 January, had in some places become a rather neglected Red Letter day in the Church's calendar. Now that CW allows it to be transferred to the Sunday between 2 and 8 January, not the preceding Sunday as Kennedy maintains (Kennedy 2006: pp. 99–100), although in most years it will lose its distinctive chronological place within the Christmas cycle because it will not follow Twelfth Night, the permission to keep it on a Sunday does provide the opportunity for the whole worshipping community to celebrate the new and radiant vision of God's glory revealed to the Magi and to the whole created order. That said, in places where a significant proportion of the Sunday assembly are likely to come to church on a weekday to celebrate one of the Church's major festivals, this is still to be preferred.

TS provides a complete order of service for the Epiphany Eucharist (pp. 159–69). The church's best white or gold vestments should be worn and the president should wear a chasuble throughout, unless there is to be a procession round the church at the beginning of the service (see below). As at Christmas, in churches where incense is only used occasionally this is certainly one of the occasions when its use should be encouraged. Indeed, even in places where incense is not ordinarily used at the Eucharist, because of its association with one of the gifts offered to the Christ-child, consideration might be given to using it on this one festival in the year.

In TS there are two distinctive features of this celebration: the offering of gifts at the crib and a dismissal Gospel. It is suggested that the offering of gifts may take place between the Gospel reading and the sermon. Alternatively, they may be offered as part of the entrance procession, while a station is made at the crib during a break in the hymn; or at the Dismissal, before the blessing. Whenever they are offered, consideration needs to be given to what form they should take. Gold might be represented by a piece of church plate or a bag of coins; incense spooned or poured into a bowl containing hot charcoal might represent frankincense; and a cruet containing the oil of the sick could symbolize myrrh. In many communities it will be appropriate to involve children in the preparation and offering of the gifts. Alternatively, TS suggests that, instead of the offering of gifts, figures of the wise men might be placed in the crib. Indeed, there would be no harm in doing both at the same time, the Magi also being presented by children. If the Magi are not placed in the crib during the liturgy, they should be put into position before the service starts.

The Gathering

If gifts are to be offered at the crib and/or figures of the Magi are to be placed in it, they may be carried by children or others in the entrance procession, preceding the sacred ministers. When the procession reaches the sanctuary, the president may receive the gifts and/or figures from the children and place them on the altar, or on a table in front of it, before the altar is censed.

Alternatively, in churches where it is customary on major festivals to begin the Eucharist with a procession round the church, as encouraged by Dearmer (Dearmer 1932: pp. 254–64), the ministers should proceed directly to the sanctuary, the president wearing a cope. Incense is put on. The organist plays the introduction to the (first) processional hymn. The deacon, president or another minister sings, 'Let us proceed in peace', to which the response is made, **'In the name of Christ. Amen'**, and the hymn begins as the procession moves round the church, often in the pattern of a 'figure of eight'. The congregation should be encouraged to join in this procession, following the ministers. Banners may also be carried by members of the congregation or servers. Although not included in all hymn books, 'We Three Kings' is an obvious processional hymn on this feast. If musical resources allow, the kings' parts may be sung by solo voices, the soloists either walking in the procession with the children carrying their gifts and/or figures, or singing from the pulpit or lectern. Depending on the size of the building, more than one processional hymn may be required, or the organist may improvise between verses. When the procession returns to the sanctuary, the president may receive the gifts and/or figures from the children, as described above, before censing the altar. The cope should be changed for the chasuble before the president greets the people.

In TS a versicle and response, based on Malachi 1.11, may precede the greeting (p. 159). Bearing in mind the general convention, referred to in the previous chapter, that the greeting should be the president's first words to the people, it may be more desirable for this acclamation, if used, to follow the greeting, rather than precede it, particularly if another minister leads the introduction to the Prayers of Penitence. Although, in TS, the *Gloria in Excelsis* is optional, it would not be appropriate to omit this canticle on a Principal Feast.

The Liturgy of the Word

TS suggests that the Gospel may be read from the crib before the gifts of the wise men are presented. To follow this suggestion, a procession could be formed after the second reading and, even if a gradual hymn is not normally sung before the Gospel, one would be appropriate on this occasion. The president may hand the gifts and/or figures to the children to carry to the crib, following the thurifer and acolytes, and preceding the ministers. The deacon or another minister should carry the Gospel Book, and the congregation should be encouraged to gather round the crib or, at least, turn to face it. If the hymn is long enough, half of it may be sung during the procession to the crib and the second half on the way back. Alternatively, if 'We Three Kings' is sung here, the first verse and chorus may be used as the procession moves to the crib, the verses relating to each of the Magi and their gifts before their respective gifts are presented, and the final verse as the procession returns. If it is desired to use the Gospel acclamation, this should be sung immediately before the Gospel reading, and may still be sung even if it occurs after a break in the middle of a hymn. The Gospel should be proclaimed in the usual way, the Gospel Book being censed after it has been announced, and then each of the gifts (with their figures) may be presented by the children, perhaps kneeling momentarily before doing so, the president saying the appropriate *berakah* prayer as each gift is placed in, or in front of, the crib; or, in the case of the incense, burnt in a bowl.

If an informal address follows, perhaps based around the significance of the gifts, it may be appropriate, as Kennedy suggests (Kennedy 2006: p. 108), for this to take place at the crib. Although Kennedy proposes that the prayers of intercession may also be led from the crib, since the Epiphany is a Principal Feast, the Nicene Creed should not be omitted, and so it may be more appropriate for the congregation and ministers to return to their places, either after the presentation of gifts or after the sermon.

The Liturgy of the Sacrament

The Liturgy of the Sacrament proceeds as usual. As noted in CCW2, if gifts have been presented, the use of the second prayer at the Preparation of the Table 'which says that the people's gifts are "not gold, frankincense and myrrh, but hearts and voices raised in praise", although of course true at one level, might nevertheless seem strange put in those terms' (CCW2 2006: p. 77). Such an apparent contradiction could well be addressed in the sermon, or in a note introducing the service, printed at the beginning of the order of service.

TS prints three possible proper prefaces to be used in the Eucharistic Prayer, two short and one extended (p. 166). Although the extended preface gives thanks for the three events celebrated at Epiphany – the coming of the Magi, the baptism of Christ and the miracle at Cana – on the Feast of the Epiphany itself, where the focus is on the Magi and the crib, one of the short prefaces is probably most appropriate.

The Dismissal

The Dismissal in TS contains four elements: a responsive acclamation, the dismissal Gospel (Luke 2.28–32), the blessing and the final dismissal. The acclamation introduces an appropriate note of praise and thanksgiving at the end of the Eucharist which mirrors the opening acclamation. Divided into three sections, each may be led by one of the children who presented the gifts earlier in the service. With the dismissal Gospel, the worshipper is taken from the crib to the temple, to hear Simeon's song of encounter and farewell, the *Nunc dimittis.* Although, in CW, the Presentation of Christ in the Temple marks the end of the Christmas/Epiphany season, to anticipate the bitter/sweet taste of that festival on the Feast of the Epiphany seems incongruous and is probably best omitted, particularly since similar sentiments have traditionally been associated with the gift of myrrh which, in the words of 'Bethlehem, of Noblest Cities', 'a future tomb foreshows'.

The Eucharist on the Festival of the Baptism of Christ

The celebration of the Festival of the Baptism of Christ on the First Sunday of Epiphany (or the Second Sunday of Epiphany, if the 6 January is itself the First Sunday; or on Monday 8 or 9 January if Epiphany is celebrated on Sunday 7 or 8 January; see TS: p. 26) provides not only a suitable occasion for the celebration of baptism (and confirmation), but also an opportunity for members of the local community to give thanks for the sacrament of baptism and, recalling their own baptismal promises, rededicate their lives to God in penitence and in faith. TS offers a fully worked-out order for a service which includes an act of thanksgiving for baptism between the Liturgy of the Word and the Liturgy of the Eucharist (pp. 172–83), together with the outline structure of a service in which, instead of the rite of thanksgiving, baptism itself is celebrated (pp. 170–1).

It is interesting to note that the Thanksgiving for Baptism, which takes place at the font, does not include the renewal of baptismal vows. It has three elements: a prayer over the water, an optional chant or acclamation, and an act of penitence and dedication (TS: 175–7). Although this form is entirely fitting for this festival, it is also an appropriate occasion for the renewal of baptismal promises, as *Common Worship: Christian Initiation* (hereafter CI) acknowledges (CI: p. 193, note 1). The Form for the Corporate Renewal of Baptismal Vows (CI: pp. 193–5) can easily replace the act of penitence and dedication in TS, the congregation being sprinkled after the profession of faith. If baptism is celebrated within the context of this service, the congregation may renew their promises by joining the candidate(s) in making the decision, as well as the profession of faith, as at the Easter Vigil (TS: pp. 342–4). For further comment on the celebration of baptism on this festival, see Chapter 7.

However the rite is celebrated, if part of the liturgy is to take place at the font, the Paschal Candle should be lit throughout the service. If desired, hand-held candles could be given to members of the congregation and lit for the renewal of baptismal vows, a symbol of the light of Christ which Christians receive in baptism.

As far as vesture is concerned, white is the liturgical colour for this festival, and the president should wear a white chasuble throughout the rite.

The Gathering

In the entrance procession, it would be appropriate for a ewer of water to be carried in front of the ministers, preferably by a member of the congregation in lay dress. On reaching the sanctuary, it may be placed in front of the altar, or in a position where it remains visible to the congregation. As with the Epiphany order, a versicle and response based on Malachi 1.11 may be said before the president's greeting. The desirability of such an acclamation has already been questioned (see p. 55). Again, like the Epiphany order, TS indicates that the *Gloria in Excelsis* is optional. Since the Baptism of Christ is a Festival which nearly always falls on a Sunday, the *Gloria* should always be used. In this rite, as the penitential material occurs as part of the Thanksgiving for Baptism, there are no Prayers of Penitence within the Gathering. Rather, the president's welcome and introduction to the liturgy may be structured in such a way as to lead straight into the *Gloria*, the Collect for Purity being omitted. For example:

A voice from heaven said: 'This is my Son, the beloved,
with whom I am well pleased.'
As today we celebrate the baptism of Jesus,
let us rejoice that, in baptism, we have become the Father's
beloved children,
and so give glory to God in the highest.

Thanksgiving for Holy Baptism

After the sermon, the ewer of water should be taken in procession to the font, led by cross and lights. The ministers follow and the congregation should be encouraged to gather round or, at least, turn to face the font. A suitable hymn, chant or the litany of the saints may accompany the procession. If the hymn is long enough, it may be broken in half, the second portion being sung as the procession returns to the sanctuary. TS provides a form of words which may be said as the water is poured into the font. It would be appropriate for the person carrying the water to pour it while the response is led by the president. As at baptism, the water should be poured in from a height so that it is clearly visible to the congregation (for further discussion of this, see CCW1: pp. 166–7). The Prayer over the Water which follows is the Epiphany text from CI. After the two responses, the president's hands may be raised in the *orans* position. At the words, 'May your holy and life-giving Spirit move upon these waters', the hands may be lowered, as at the epiclesis in the Eucharistic Prayer; then, as the prayer continues, the sign of the cross may be made in the water. The *orans* position should be adopted again for the remainder of the prayer, with the hands coming together for the final doxology.

The suggested sung acclamation which follows begins with the words of the *Vidi aquam* ('I saw water': Ezekiel 47.1), a chant traditionally sung in place of the *Asperges me*, during the sprinkling at the beginning of Mass during Eastertide in the Roman rite. Where musical resources allow, it would be appropriate for the *Vidi aquam* to be sung here. Alternatively, there are a number of possible congregational hymns, songs and chants which may be used, among them:

'Water of Life' (*New English Praise*, 655)
'With Joy You Will Draw Water' (*New English Praise*, 690)
'Spirit of the Living God' (*Hymns Old & New*, 454)

The act of penitence and dedication which follows is heavy on penitence (with the response 'From all our sins, O Lord: **wash us, and we shall be clean**' being used after each section) but regrettably rather light on expressing rededication, with the exception of one petition in the final prayer, 'May we, whom you have counted worthy, nurture your indwelling Spirit with a lively faith, and worship you with upright lives.' This is perhaps a reason why the renewal of baptismal vows might be more appropriate on this feast. Where it is used, the leading of the act of penitence and dedication may be divided between several ministers.

It is followed by sprinkling with baptismal water or, alternatively, members of the congregation may come forward and sign themselves with the water from the font. Sprinkling is preferable, particularly with a large congregation. Although an aspergilium may be used for this purpose, sprinkling with a large sprig of rosemary, or several pieces bound together, allows the sprinkling to be smelled as well as felt. A suitable hymn, chant or song may accompany the sprinkling, such as those already referred to. Some of the music intended for the renewal of baptismal vows at the Easter Vigil is also appropriate. For example, the following verse sung to the tune *Lasst uns erfreuen*:

Come, flowing waters, pure and clear,
God's Holy Spirit bringing near,
Let us praise him, alleluia!
Join each to each in peace and love,
with life you give us from above.
O praise him, O praise him,
alleluia, alleluia, alleluia.
(Dean 1992: p. 105)

The president concludes the thanksgiving with a final prayer for forgiveness, said with hands joined, before the procession returns to the sanctuary. Alternatively, the Peace could follow immediately and the procession return during the offertory hymn.

The Dismissal

The structure of the Dismissal is identical to that on the Feast of the Epiphany and other dismissal rites in TS: acclamation, dismissal Gospel, blessing and dismissal. On this festival, it may be appropriate for this final part of the service to take place at the font. The final hymn could be sung after the prayer after Communion, during which the procession could move to the font, a minister carrying the Gospel Book. Incense could lead the procession and be used to cense the book after the Gospel has been announced. The blessing and dismissal follow. On leaving the church, members of the congregation could be encouraged to sign themselves with water from the font, perhaps taking away a card marking the occasion and containing the words of the Apostles' Creed, the baptismal profession of faith, and a prayer for the baptized members of the local community as well as those who will be baptized in the coming year, their godparents and sponsors.

A Service for the Festival of the Baptism of Christ

A revised version of a service first published in PHG, this liturgy has much creative potential. It celebrates the three 'wonders' of Epiphany: the visit of the Magi, the Baptism of Christ and the miracle at Cana to 'form an Epiphany Procession or Epiphany Carol Service, at the climax of which is the Renewal of the Covenant or of baptismal vows' (TS: p. 185, note 2). Although primarily intended for use on the Festival of the Baptism of Christ, TS suggests that it may also be used at the Epiphany itself, on the eve of the Epiphany, or on any suitable occasion between Epiphany and Candlemas (p. 185, note 1). Designed as a non-eucharistic service, note 3 explains how the material provided can be combined with a celebration of the Eucharist, particularly if the celebration of the miracle at Cana acts as a bridge between the renewal of the covenant and the Liturgy of the Sacrament. That said, since TS provides fully worked-out eucharistic rites for Epiphany and the Baptism of Christ, it is perhaps most likely to be used as a non-eucharistic evening service. Indeed, when considering what liturgical provision would be most suited for this festival, it should be borne in mind that the use of two 'water rites' on one day, even on this particular day, runs the risk of diminishing their significance for a particular community, unless the morning and evening services are attended by different congregations, or the morning Eucharist is celebrated by the local congregation and the evening service is a deanery, archdeaconry or diocesan occasion.

Movement is a key feature of this service, and people's engagement with the liturgy will be impoverished if its performance is static. Although, as note 4 makes clear, the way in which the rite is celebrated will vary from church to church and depend on the position of the crib, the font and the altar, each focal point should, if possible, have its own space to which people are able to move and around which they can gather. Since in many churches the crib and the font are in close proximity to each other, TS suggests that a bowl of water may be set up in the middle of the church for the Prayer over the Water, and carried from there to the font at the end of the service (p. 185, note 4).

If celebrated as a deanery, archdeaconry or diocesan occasion, it would be appropriate for the bishop to preside over the service, delegating various elements within the rite to other ministers and members of the assembly. The acclamations which introduce each of the 'epiphanies' and the Gospel readings proclaiming them are particularly suited to the ministry of deacons. White is the liturgical colour for this celebration. The officiant may wear a cope, and a dalmatic would be appropriate vesture for any deacons. The Paschal Candle may be lit throughout the celebration.

Introduction

An acclamation praising the three 'wonders' of the Epiphany begins the service. This should be led by a minister other than the president, or someone from the congregation, standing in a prominent position such as the pulpit or lectern. An opening hymn such as 'Songs of Thankfulness and Praise', which names each of the 'wonders', would work particularly well as the servers, choir and ministers enter the assembly. Cross and lights should lead the procession. If incense is to be used during the service, it may be saved for the proclamation of the 'wonders' and need not be carried here. Any robed ministers should follow the choir, and the deacon, or deacons, should precede the officiant, one of them carrying the Book of the Gospels.

The president may introduce the rite from the chair, or from wherever the Gathering is normally led at the Eucharist. As at the Eucharist, the Trinitarian acclamation may preface the greeting. If the president is a bishop the apostolic greeting, 'Peace be with you', would be appropriate. During the opening prayer, and at each of the prayers following the Gospel readings, the president should adopt the *orans* position and, as at the collect, a brief period of silence should be kept after the invitation to pray before the prayer itself is said or sung.

As the liturgy is presented in TS, there is very little opportunity for the congregation to sit, except where carols are sung by the choir. Although not suggested in TS, a carol could be sung after the opening prayer before the first 'wonder' is celebrated.

The King of all the world is revealed to the Magi

The deacon or other minister announcing the first 'wonder' should stand in the same prominent place from which the introductory acclamation was made and, if possible, should be the same person who will proclaim the Gospel from the crib. So that the gifts are not brought up in silence, they may be brought forward during the responsory, or while a short carol is sung. TS notes that the gifts presented may be any one or all of the traditional gifts (p. 185, note 6), to which reference has already been made. Alternatively, TS suggests that the Christmas collections may be presented. While this may be appropriate if they have been collected for a particular charity, as is common at Christmas, it is less so if they are for the general running expenses of the parish, when the sense of sacrificial giving is not as strong. A procession is formed which leads the gifts and ministers to the crib while a hymn, preferably an Epiphany hymn, is sung. Where possible, the choir should be part of the procession, and the congregation should follow. If large numbers of people are present, or if space is limited, it should, at least, be possible for people to turn towards the crib as the Gospel is proclaimed. Incense, imposed and blessed by the president, may lead the procession, and the deacon or other minister reading the Gospel should carry the Gospel Book, and may ask a blessing from the president before the procession begins. Before the Gospel is proclaimed, the Gospel Book may be censed, as at the Eucharist.

At the end of the Gospel, the deacon should kiss the book or, if the president is a bishop, the book should be offered to him to kiss. He may also close the book and bless the congregation with it, wearing the mitre and making the sign of the cross (GIRM: 175). The gifts are placed before the crib and the president concludes this part of the rite with the collect of the Epiphany. If carols are to follow, consideration needs to be given to allowing the congregation to sit. Christina Rossetti's 'In the Bleak Midwinter' would work particularly well here.

The new creation is revealed in the water made wine

The deacon or other minister who will proclaim the next Gospel should also lead the opening acclamation and may ask a blessing from the president before carrying the Gospel Book in the procession. Incense, imposed and blessed again, may lead the procession and, if possible, the wine should be carried in a large glass cruet, rather than a flagon or chalice, so that its contents are visible. At the altar, the Gospel should be proclaimed from a central position, with the person carrying the wine standing next to the reader. Incense may be used, as before, and the bishop, if present, may once again bless the people with the Book of the Gospels before the wine is placed on the altar.

The Christ is revealed in the waters of baptism

Another minister leads the opening acclamation as water is brought forward in a ewer, or whatever is normally used to hold the baptismal water before it is poured into the font. The procession is formed again and moves to the font. The Gospel may be proclaimed with the same ceremonial that accompanied the previous two epiphanies. On this occasion, the president's prayer follows immediately, after which the water is poured into the font. TS suggests two Prayers over the Water which may be used: a long presidential text, or a shorter responsorial form. The longer text is filled with rich imagery taken from the Byzantine tradition. If this is used, after the *Sursum corda* (during which the president may use the same gestures as at the Eucharistic Prayer) the choir or a cantor may lead the congregation in the singing of a simple chant, such as the Taizé *Veni, sancte Spiritus*, which may be sung softly as the president offers the prayer. The president may divide the prayer into several parts and pause at the end of each, during which the cantor or choir may sing appropriate verses over the chant, which should stop after the final petition, 'and serve you in newness of life', so that everyone is able to join in the response to the doxology.

As in the eucharistic liturgy for this day, a suitable chant or acclamation may follow the Prayer over the Water, although this won't be required if the congregation has been singing during the prayer. TS suggests that the Renewal of the Covenant, from the Methodist Covenant Service, may follow (see above, pp. 46–7). It would also be appropriate for the renewal of baptismal vows (CI: pp. 193–5) to take place here. Although TS suggests that prayers should be offered at the font before the congregation is sprinkled with baptismal water, if people have been standing for a long period of time it may make more sense to sprinkle them after the Act of Renewal, and then for a hymn to be sung while they return to their places, so that they may sit for the prayers, if necessary.

The Sending Out

A short and a solemn blessing are provided. The latter, which mentions all three 'wonders', is particularly appropriate on this occasion. If the president is a bishop, a simple greeting followed by the responses which traditionally precede an episcopal blessing (see CI: p. 130, note 13) could precede either form. A deacon or other minister should give the dismissal.

For a description of how this rite might be celebrated by a charismatic, evangelical church, see Kennedy 2006: pp. 111–13.

5

The Presentation of Christ in the Temple (Candlemas)

And now we give you thanks
because, by appearing in the Temple,
he comes near to us in judgement;
the Word made flesh searches the hearts of all your people
and brings to light the brightness of your splendour.

And now we give you thanks
because your eternal Word took our nature upon him
in the womb of Mary the Virgin.
The sword of sorrow pierced her heart
when he was lifted high on the cross,
and by his sacrifice made our peace with you.
(Short Prefaces for the Presentation, TS: p. 201)

Liturgical character

The short prefaces which may be used on the Principal Feast of the Presentation of Christ in the Temple convey the fact that, despite this title, its main emphasis is not unambiguously as a feast of the Lord: there remains a certain diversity of focus which contributes towards its richness, reflected in the various titles given to it in the Western tradition. The Gregorian Sacramentary called this day 'the Meeting' (understood to be of Simeon and the Lord), which is also its Eastern name, and the Gelasian tradition simply entitled it 'St Simeon'. Following the greater Marian emphasis of later medieval practice, BCP calls this day (albeit in translation) 'The Purification of the Virgin Mary', and the Marian flavour is by no means absent from the modern celebration. The point is not, in the end, one of exclusivity of emphasis, but the combination of themes and allusions which encapsulates the incarnation, epiphany and the passion of the Lord in a celebration which acts as a liturgical 'hinge' between Epiphany and the beginning of Lent. There is a joyful yet presciently haunting quality to the liturgy of a day which also acquired the popular name 'Candlemas' in reference to the blessing of candles which came to be associated with it.

As an occasion of joy, the church should be decorated accordingly with flowers and perhaps additional candles. By way of historical precedent for the latter in the Church of England, it is known that Bishop John Cosin of Durham (1594–1672) so decorated the cathedral for the occasion:

> On Candlemas Day last past Mr Cosens (*sic*) . . . busied himself from two of the clock in the afternoon till four climbing long ladders to stick up wax candles . . . The number of all the candles burnt that evening was 220, besides 16 torches, 60 of those burning tapers and torches standing upon and near the High Altar (as he calls it).
>
> (Peter Smart, sermon in Durham Cathedral, 27 July 1628, quoted in More and Cross 1935: p. 551)

Although Cosin's actions are reported in an original context of negative criticism, the quoting of this description in this guide is, of course, rather intended as encouragement!

The liturgical colour of the day is white or gold, but the principle of 'the best available' of whatever colour might be followed in the case of a cope for the president in the procession. This should not include purple, once worn for the Candlemas procession, since this would detract from the celebratory feel which should be present from the beginning.

Given the richness of the themes and the considerable liturgical significance of the Presentation, consideration may be given to transferring it to the nearest Sunday, as CW allows, in order to permit its celebration with the majority of the worshipping community. It must be borne in mind, however, that this will probably involve a procession with candles in daylight, whereas a weekday evening celebration would take advantage of the darkness of the time of year and provide a striking setting, reflecting the contrast of darkness and light present in the liturgy of the day.

The Liturgy of Candlemas

The Blessing of Candles

In medieval times and in some places until relatively recently 'Candlemas' was the occasion for blessing *all* the candles to be used liturgically in the coming year. This is not impossible today, but would seem largely impractical now for the simple reason that it is not usual to order an entire year's worth of candles at the same time. This is not to say, however, that candles should not feature prominently in the liturgy, and they should certainly be carried by all present.

Today it is usually only those candles to be carried in procession that are blessed. This may be done either once they have been distributed, in which case they should be held aloft, unlit, for the Prayer of Blessing and any sprinkling (and perhaps censing) that may accompany it. They should then be lit, most conveniently from the acolytes' torches, the light being passed from one person to another. Alternatively, the candles may be blessed before they are distributed, but this would seem not to be the intention of the Prayer of Blessing in TS, which incorporates those who carry the candles. If it is done this way, the candles should be distributed and lit from the acolytes' torches as before. If the procession is to take place partly outside, the problem of processing with lit candles in even the gentlest of breezes must be borne in mind. One solution is to place two lit acolyte torches in stands just inside the church door, from which individuals may relight their candles if necessary, or to assign two members of the congregation to stand there with lit candles for the same purpose. However, it would be preferable for them to be able to join the procession.

There is the practical issue of the president's candle. Because the president will need to have hands free to pray in the *orans* manner and to sprinkle and cense the candles and/or the people holding their candles (see below), a server will need to hold the president's candle when necessary, receiving it and passing it back at the appropriate moments, and perhaps also extinguishing and relighting it. The president must process with a lighted candle, which ought to be of the same size and design as those of the people. There is no merit in providing the president with a larger candle than those of everyone else.

In former times the candles held by individuals were extinguished and re-lit several times during the liturgy: lit for the procession, then extinguished; lit for the Gospel, then extinguished; lit for the Eucharistic Prayer, then extinguished. Now it is quite appropriate for the candles to remain lit throughout the liturgy as far as is possible. They should certainly remain lit at least for the procession until after the *Gloria in Excelsis*, and may be lit again during the offertory for the Eucharistic Prayer, being extinguished as people go forward to receive Holy Communion. Safety and convenience will inform the choice made in this respect, bearing in mind the practical difficulty of handling a lit candle, a hymn book and a service sheet at the same time. This suggests the production of a service sheet which contains everything needed for the celebration, including the hymns.

The Candlemas procession

The distinctive feature of this liturgy, as the TS rubric states, is the procession with lighted candles. This may occur at the beginning or end of the service, or before the Gospel, but much to be preferred is the beginning, the most traditional but also arguably the most logical and liturgically powerful position. This and the other two positions are considered below. TS provides texts for all three possibilities, but clearly favours the procession taking place at the end of the service. Each option will be examined here in chronological order, the Gathering option including some general points which apply to whichever option is used.

The procession as Gathering

In TS this is called 'Candlemas Procession earlier in the Service', and the material provided applies to both the beginning and pre-Gospel options. The welcoming of the people by the president with which the form begins, however, surely presupposes the procession taking place at the beginning of the service.

If the procession is at the beginning, it can contribute most effectively towards an extended Gathering rite if the people assemble in a separate place such as a church hall or a chapel (or perhaps at the font) and process to their places in church (as liturgical 'temple') from there, as they will do on Palm Sunday in commemoration of Jesus' solemn entry into Jerusalem. Indeed, an explicit association of these two processions may be made, since Candlemas is the liturgical 'hinge' which both looks back to the birth and forward to the passion of the Lord.

So far as is possible, the procession must include all present – it is not intended to be a procession of clergy, choir and servers only. Where there is a small building, assembling outside in the churchyard, in the street or in a hall will make possible the involvement of everyone. Those unable to walk in the procession should be shown to their places before the service and provided with a candle, where appropriate, that must be lit in time for the entry of the procession so that they may nevertheless participate in the larger import of what is happening. Elliott's advice that 'Ushers should supervise the procession and maintain due order' (Elliott 2002: p. 76) is probably unnecessary! However, given the seeming reluctance of many Anglicans to process, some gentle encouragement may help.

In a larger church with aisles, even if the people gather in the nave as normal, the procession can take an extended route around the building, perhaps but not necessarily following the traditional 'figure of eight' pattern. The important thing is the image of the people of God on pilgrimage with and to their Lord, however far or for however long they process.

The blessing of the candles and the procession used to require the priest to wear a purple stole and cope, changing to a white chasuble for the Eucharist which followed. There *is* a distinct hint of darkness as the shadow of the cross falls across the proceedings in the Temple in the Gospel account ('a sword shall pierce your own heart also'), but this speaks for itself in the proclaiming of the Gospel and can be amplified in the sermon. The procession should be one of joy reflecting the fulfilment in the presence of the Lord experienced by Simeon. Therefore the president should wear white or gold from the beginning of the liturgy.

The following order is suggested:

- Greeting.
- Blessing of candles.
- Sprinkling (and perhaps censing).
- *Nunc dimittis* as candles are lit.
- Procession with hymns (including, for example, 'Hail, to the Lord Who Comes').
- *Gloria in Excelsis* when all are in their places.

TS suggests that a procession at the beginning of the service might take place *during* the singing of *Gloria in Excelsis*, whereas 'Nunc dimittis is more suitable if the procession is made at the end of the service' (p. 206). However, the *Nunc dimittis* can be included when the procession is at the beginning of the service by adopting the order suggested above. Either the contemporary English Language Liturgical Consultation (ELLC) version or the BCP text of the *Nunc dimittis* may be used, or if necessary a hymn based on its words (for example, 'Faithful Vigil Ended').

When all are ready, the president greets the people. It would make good sense for the president then to use the introductory text provided in TS (p. 195) or to introduce the liturgy in other suitable words, even though the TS form for the procession at the beginning of the service (p. 206) does not include this.

The blessing of the candles in the form provided by TS (p. 206) is in the form of a response, a *berakah*-type prayer ('Blessed are you . . .'), and a prayer of blessing. TS assumes them to have been already lit, but this need not be the case, if following the order suggested above. The words 'bless these candles' might be added to the text of the blessing prayer, as follows:

> Lord God, the springing source of everlasting light,
> \+ *bless these candles, and* pour into the hearts of your faithful
>   people
> the brilliance of your eternal splendour,
> that we, who by these kindling flames
> light up this temple to your glory,
> may have the darkness of our souls dispelled,
> and so be counted worthy to stand before you
> in that eternal city where you live and reign,
> Father, Son and Holy Spirit,
> one God, now and for ever.
> **Amen.**

After the prayer of blessing, the people and their candles are sprinkled with water by the president who moves around and/or among them to reach as many as possible. The president then censes the people in the same way. The candles are then lit as *Nunc dimittis* is sung. The acolytes need to stand in such a place as to make possible the simple sharing of the light from their torches; members of the congregation can be assigned to light their candles first from the torches and then pass the flame to others.

A set of responses may follow (TS: p. 206). Unlike Palm Sunday, in TS there is no specific invitation to process (such as, 'Let us go forth . . .'). The Roman Rite supplies 'Let us go in peace to meet the Lord' (WM: p. 1404).

The order of the procession should typically be: thurifer, acolytes and crucifer, choir, other servers, MC, readers, assisting clergy (who may be concelebrants), subdeacon (in churches where this is the custom), deacon (or Gospeller in priest's orders), president, people. Alternatively, the people may follow the choir; this would allow most of them to be in their places by the time the sanctuary party processes through the church. It is not necessary for people to walk in neat pairs, unless a particularly narrow aisle compels it.

The procession before the Gospel

The TS material for a 'Candlemas procession earlier in the service' (pp. 206–7) may also be used for a procession before the Gospel, but without the opening words of greeting. In this case, the *Gloria in Excelsis* having been sung as part of the Gathering, the singing of 'Hail, to the Lord Who Comes' during the procession is suggested; in tone it could be said to be an extended Gospel acclamation. Here again, there is the possibility of singing *Nunc dimittis* at the end of the service.

The option in TS to place the procession before the Gospel, however, has the danger of overshadowing the proclamation of the Gospel itself. If this option is taken, the procession must be obviously distinct from the normal Gospel procession if the message of the distinctive rites of this day is to be conveyed. In a large church, it may be done in such a way that the Candlemas procession becomes the Gospel procession. This will mean people leaving their places, and thought must be given to where the Gospel should be read from. The simplest solution is to plan the procession in such a way as to end up with the Gospel being read from the usual place, whether at the ambo, at the chancel step, or in the nave. A more imaginative solution would be to process to the font, the place of purification in the waters of baptism, and have the Gospel read from there with the people gathered round. The practicality of this interpretation will of course depend on the position of the font. It must be borne in mind, though, that the font may well have played a prominent part in the liturgy for the Baptism of Christ; to use it here in this way might seem too similar or repetitious.

The procession before the Dismissal

The choosing of this option, the preferred one in TS, might at first seem the most appropriate to the text of the *Nunc dimittis*, sung during, before or after the procession: 'Lord, now you let your servant depart in peace', and this is the implication of a TS rubric (p. 206). The material provided for the procession at the end of the service is given in two alternative forms. In the first (p. 203) the prayer of blessing begins the rite, the candles having been distributed (and presumably lit) during a hymn. The destination of the procession might be 'the font . . . the door of the church, or another suitable place' (p. 203). The *Nunc dimittis* in any suitable form follows (a responsive example in contemporary English and the BCP text are given in TS). On this occasion it would be appropriate to use a form that enabled all to join in the singing of the canticle, to correspond with the procession for all. There is a lengthy final responsory (p. 204) which is only suitable for the very end of the service. The Alternative Candlemas Procession (p. 205) is wholly responsive in form. The equivalent of the prayer of blessing could be transposed to a procession earlier in the service, but the Final Responsory and Conclusion can only be used at the end of the service.

An alternative to this option might be sought if it is argued that use of the *Nunc dimittis* in this way at the end of the service takes these words of Simeon out of context on the grounds of superficial similarity to the present action of the congregation. There is much to be said for the notion of departing having met the Lord in the Eucharist in the 'temple' of the church building, as Simeon met his Lord in the Temple. For the Christian, though, the sense of movement is always that of pilgrimage towards the Lord who meets us in the Eucharist and who is present in us and in the faces of one another. He is not 'left behind' at the end of the Eucharist, in order to be encountered again only there, but is present in the world and its daily life. 'Departing in peace' certainly echoes the words of the Dismissal, but ought not to have the sense of finality, the life fulfilled at its end, which it has in respect of Simeon. The encounter with the Lord of the Eucharist in the Temple of the Church is a new beginning, a re-presentation of the one sacrifice alluded to in the Gospel of the day and to which the baptized are already indelibly united. On this understanding, 'departure' is misleading when the people of God are going to greet the Lord in their daily lives, for which they nevertheless and necessarily 'Go in peace'.

The Gathering

It is recommended that the procession form the principal element of the Gathering, as explained above. When all are in their places after the procession, Prayers of Penitence may follow, although as an alternative TS suggests placing them later in the liturgy, after the intercessions. There is something to be said for the procession to be immediately followed by the *Gloria in Excelsis* (see above), which must be sung on this feast as the song of the angels alluding to the dimension of 'looking back' to the nativity and epiphany of the Lord, whereas the Gospel will allude to his passion yet to come in liturgical time. An alternative to the *Gloria* is the hymn 'Angels from the Realms of Glory', particularly appropriate since it contains the verse 'Saints before the altar bending . . . in his Temple shall appear'.

The Liturgy of the Word

Three readings with the accompanying psalmody are preferable. The people's candles should be lit for the Gospel, and extinguished for the sermon. A sermon should be preached on this richly scriptural and liturgical occasion, drawing especial attention to the bidirectional perspectives back to Christmas and Epiphany and forward to Lent and Passiontide. An authorized affirmation of faith must be used since this is a Principal Feast. The intercessions might use the set provided in TS, or be locally composed, but must not be of the same nature in terms of style and content as those at a Sunday Parish Eucharist. Rather, they should encapsulate and intercede in definite relation to the themes of the feast. It would be an appropriate occasion for the use of the 'Hail Mary'. The relatively brief set in TS are appropriate for use when the Prayers of Penitence follow.

The Liturgy of the Sacrament

The hand-held candles may be re-lit for the Eucharistic Prayer, to be extinguished as people come forward to receive Communion. The extended preface for this day is preferable if the richness of its character is to be continued; it makes particular reference to the passion as earlier alluded to in the Gospel. The two short prefaces divide between them the backwards and forwards perspectives, whereas the extended preface obviates the need to make a choice.

The Dismissal

The Final Responsory makes effective use of the double-edged nature of the celebration in looking back and forwards, as mentioned above, in particular 'Here we turn from Christ's birth to his passion'. While intended to conclude the procession when this takes place at the end of the service, the responsory could nevertheless be used as part of an extended dismissal rite.

In some communities it may be appropriate to say or sing the *Angelus* after the Dismissal, or incorporate it in the dismissal rite so as not to create the impression of 'Go, but not before we have sung this'.

The 'Alternative Candlemas Procession' for use at the end of the service in TS (p. 205) suggests the lighting of the candles during the singing of a hymn, with the prayer of blessing interspersed with the response 'Blessed be God for ever'. The procession then moves 'to the font, or to the door of the church, or to another suitable place' (TS: p. 205), during which *Nunc dimittis* or a hymn is sung. A suggested option is the placing of a 'large cross' at the destination of the procession. If that destination is the font, it could be argued that no further symbol is required, but it may be felt that the cross usefully points towards the coming season of Lent, a visual expression of that characteristic of the Gospel reading. To these suggestions in TS could be added the ritual extinguishing of the candles at the conclusion of the service, with the implication that the light of Christ is in the people themselves, to be carried into and shared in the world.

Between the Presentation and Lent

In years when Easter is very early (as in 2008), there might be a very short period of Ordinary Time between the Presentation and Ash Wednesday, possibly made even shorter by the transfer of the former to the nearest Sunday. There is no solution to this apparent oddity where it occurs, but a positive interpretation is that it is a reminder that human organization of time is ultimately subject to the God who is Lord of time, recalling Aidan Kavanagh's comment that 'liturgy needs time rather than time needs liturgy' (Kavanagh 1992: p. 24). The point is in the seeming inconsistency and untidiness – the result of the very human attempt to organize time that established the complex formula for the calculation of the date of Easter while leaving Christmas as a fixed date. As Thomas Merton remarked, the liturgical year is indeed 'humanly insecure'.

6

All Saints to Advent

And now we give you thanks
that he is the King of glory,
who overcomes the sting of death
and opens the kingdom of heaven to all believers.
He is seated at your right hand in glory
and we believe that he will come to be our judge.
(Short Preface from All Saints to Advent, TS: p. 544)

Liturgical character

It has been said of November that it is 'the month of the dead', but this should not be interpreted negatively or joylessly. Observed on successive days, All Saints and All Souls are, at their heart, ecclesiological and eschatological observances, encouraging the Christian community to reflect on what it means to belong to a worshipping community which, united in its worship of the King of glory, spans both heaven and earth. The fellowship of the saints in heaven is a source of constant encouragement to those who journey towards the judgement seat of Christ; the prayers of the Church on earth unite its desire with the Father's desire that the departed may come to enjoy eternal peace in the kingdom which his Son has opened to all believers. To articulate this sense of belonging, these commemorations enable Christian believers to celebrate their membership of the communion of saints, give thanks for those whose lives have been recognized as reflecting the grace and truth of God in an exemplary way, and commend to God in prayer those whose journey is now separated from ours by the 'narrow stream of death', to use Wesley's words.

Following the lead of PHG, CW has turned the period from All Saints to Advent into a quasi-season. While PHG went as far as to refer to this period as the 'Kingdom season', CW defines it as a 'time to celebrate and reflect upon the reign of Christ in heaven and on earth' within Ordinary Time. That said, the optional use of red rather than green as the liturgical colour does gives these weeks before Advent, which also embrace Remembrance Sunday and the Feast of Christ the King, their own liturgical identity. Although some may wish to mark out this 'season' in this way, red's well-established association with the Holy Spirit, the passion of Christ and martyrdom, makes it a somewhat surprising choice.

However it is observed, this 'season' begins with the first Evening Prayer of All Saints (whether kept on 31 October or on the eve of All Saints' Sunday) and ends before Evening Prayer on the eve of Advent Sunday.

The Eucharist of All Saints

TS provides a fully worked-out order of service for the principal celebration of All Saints, whether it takes place on All Saints' Day (1 November) or on All Saints' Sunday (falling between 30 October and 5 November). Unlike Epiphany which, if transferred to the nearest Sunday, is not observed at all on 6 January, the CW calendar permits a 'secondary celebration' of All Saints on 1 November, if it is transferred (TS: p. 24). CW also provides readings for the Principal Service on All Saints for each of the three years of the lectionary, together with an additional set which may be used on 1 November if All Saints is kept on the Sunday.

The Church's best white or gold vestments should be used for this Eucharist and, unless there is to be a festival procession round the church at the beginning of the service (see below), the president should wear a chasuble throughout the rite.

The Gathering

The service may begin in one of two ways: either the servers, choir and ministers process to the sanctuary as at a normal Sunday Eucharist, or if it is customary on major festivals to begin the Eucharist with a procession round the church, a practice which seems highly desirable on a feast like All Saints, the instructions given above for the procession at the beginning of the Epiphany Eucharist may be followed (see pp. 54–5). When the procession returns to the sanctuary the president censes the altar and then changes the cope for the chasuble before greeting the people.

William Walsham How's 'For All the Saints' is an obvious choice for an entrance or processional hymn on this festival and, depending on the layout of the building, it may be possible for the hymn to be broken while a station is made at an image or icon of the church's patron saint. The president leads a versicle and response and says a suitable prayer before the image, which is then censed before the procession continues. In cathedrals and greater churches which contain a shrine of their patron (such as, for example, the shrine of St Cuthbert in Durham Cathedral), this would be an appropriate location for such an act of devotion, thus enabling the worshipping community to highlight one of the saints with which it has a particular affinity within the general celebration of All Saints.

If an entrance procession is preferred to a festival procession round the church, this may be prefaced by the acclamation, 'Rejoice people of God, praise the Lord! . . .' which TS (p. 548) prints after the president's greeting. If used before the entry of the ministers, it could be read by a member of the congregation from the lectern or pulpit. Alternatively, if a station is made at an image or shrine, the same text could be used as a versicle and response before an appropriate prayer, such as the collect of the saint, is said or sung:

President	Rejoice, people of God, praise the Lord!
All	**Let us keep the feast in honour of all God's saints, in whose victory the angels rejoice and glorify the Son of God.**

The Gathering continues in the usual way and TS suggests a form of penitence which may be used on this occasion. Also suggested is the singing of the Beatitudes in place of the *Gloria in Excelsis*. This is considered particularly appropriate in Year B since, whereas the Matthean and Lukan versions of the Beatitudes are appointed as the Gospel reading in Years A and C respectively, the Year B Gospel is part of the account of the raising of Lazarus (John 11.32–44). While the Beatitudes could be sung instead of the *Gloria*, since the Beatitudes are not a song of praise, their use in this position is questionable. It could be used more appropriately to introduce the Prayers of

Penitence, as suggested in the Eucharistic rite (CWMV: p. 272), or sung as a canticle between the first two readings.

The Liturgy of the Word

On this Principal Feast, it is appropriate for two readings and a psalm or canticle to be used before the Gospel reading. The Nicene Creed should also be said.

A form of intercessions is suggested. In the final paragraph, although no provision is made for the commemoration of the church's patron saint, it could easily be adapted, as follows:

> We give you thanks
> for the Blessed Virgin Mary, for *N* our patron,
> and the whole company of your saints in glory,
> with whom in fellowship we join our prayers and praises;
> by your grace may we, like them, be made perfect in your love.

Alternatively, this would be a suitable occasion to use the 'Hail Mary' within the Prayers of Intercession, even if this is not customary. For example:

> We give you thanks
> for *N* our patron and for the whole company of your saints in glory.
> Rejoicing in their fellowship
> we ask for the prayers of Mary, first among the saints,
> as we greet her and say:
> **Hail Mary . . .**

The intercessor should then introduce a period of silent prayer before the president says a concluding collect (for example, CWMV: p. 289, prayer 5) or all join together in the doxology, '**Blessing and glory and wisdom . . .**' (TS: p. 552).

The Liturgy of the Sacrament

When deciding which Eucharistic Prayer should be used on this festival, it is worth noting that prayers B and E allow a proper preface to be used at the beginning of the prayer, and the saints to be commemorated before the final doxology. As noted in ALG 3, in the penultimate paragraph of either prayer 'all the saints and holy ones of God' may appropriately replace 'all the saints' on All Saints' Day (p. 71).

The Dismissal

TS suggests that an acclamation and dismissal Gospel (John 17.6–9) may precede the final blessing and dismissal. Whether or not the dismissal Gospel is used, All Saints' Day is an appropriate occasion for a Solemn *Te Deum* to be sung as part of the Dismissal, particularly with the canticle's reference to 'the glorious company of the apostles, the noble fellowship of the prophets and the white-robed army of martyrs'. (For further guidance on the 'solemn' use of this canticle, see Minchno 1998: p. 145). If used, a short hymn could be sung after the post-Communion prayer(s) to allow the ministers and servers to form up west of the altar, facing east; alternatively, this movement could be accompanied by a short organ improvisation. Incense should be put on by the president, and the thurible swung by the thurifer, across the body, throughout the singing of the canticle. Before the canticle begins, the acclamation (TS: p. 526) could be led by the president. Unless the musical setting precludes it, the canticle should end at verse 18 ('bring us with your saints to glory everlasting'), after which the president should turn to the congregation and give the blessing, unless the dismissal Gospel is to be proclaimed first. Although older ceremonial guides suggested that the *Te Deum*, sung *after* the Dismissal, was extra-liturgical and therefore required the president to change out of the chasuble and into a cope, when it is sung within the dismissal rite the change in vesture is not necessary.

Thanksgiving for the Holy Ones of God

This litany (TS: pp. 558–60) is, in a sense, an Anglican alternative to the Roman Catholic Litany of Saints which is used, among other occasions, to accompany the procession to the font at the Easter Vigil. As its name implies, the form provided in TS gives thanks for, rather than invokes the prayers of, the holy ones of God; and, indeed, the list of those for whom thanksgiving is offered is not restricted to those who have been canonized by the Western Church, but draws on the wider range of men and women commemorated in the CW calendar as well as certain figures from the Old Testament.

TS suggests occasions when this litany might be used: at Morning or Evening Prayer from All Saints to Advent and at services of Christian initiation in procession to or from the font. At BCP Evensong, this litany could be sung in procession at some point after the third collect, in place of the occasional prayers. In more informal settings, such as a small group celebrating Evening Prayer on a weekday, thanksgiving could be combined with intercession by selecting a few biddings, and leaving space after each for free prayer, related to the particular thanksgiving, to be offered. For example, having given thanks for 'Anselm, Richard Hooker and all who reveal the depths of God's wisdom', prayer could be offered for local schools, for all who teach religious studies, and for members of the community involved in courses of study.

To enable the litany to relate to the local as well as the universal Church, additional biddings and names may be incorporated into the second part of the litany, after the rubric, so that holy men and women who are remembered in a particular locality, or named in a diocesan calendar, are included. Where it is decided to omit certain sections, care needs to be taken so that there remains a fairly broad coverage of those who come from different periods in the history of the church as well as those who represent different categories of holiness (i.e. martyrs, evangelists, those who work for social justice, etc.).

The Eucharist of the Commemoration of the Faithful Departed (All Souls' Day)

It is not such a distant memory that the liturgical observance of All Souls' Day was the almost exclusive preserve of Anglo-Catholic communities which would celebrate a Requiem Mass on 2 November. In the last two decades, the pastoral desire to provide an opportunity for the bereaved to remember departed loved ones within the context of an act of worship which combined an authentic expression of grief with a confident proclamation of resurrection hope, has led a number of parishes of different traditions to develop an All Souls' service. This is often an evening service on the nearest Sunday, to which are often invited those who have been recently bereaved, the majority of whom will not be regular churchgoers. Although many of these services are non-Eucharistic, for Anglican Catholics there can be no substitute for celebrating a Eucharist on this day of solemn commemoration; for there is no better 'context in which the unity of the living and the departed in the body of the risen Christ is both celebrated and proclaimed' (PHG: p. 47).

CW suggests no fewer than three liturgical colours which may be used for All Souls. Purple is 'recommended', but black or white may also be used (CWMV: p. 533). For those who opt for red in the period between All Saints and Advent, Kennedy also suggests red as a possibility on this day (Kennedy 2006: p. 45). While such a choice would help to identify this particular commemoration as part of the pre-Advent 'season', there is a sense in which both All Saints and All Souls need to stand out from the weeks which follow them, as well as being easily distinguished from each other. Although both celebrate a 'mutual belonging' within the communion of saints (TS: p. 537), it is important not to underestimate the depth of grief which the liturgy of All Souls must be able to express. In a rite which is very confident in its verbal articulation of resurrection hope, the use of purple or black vestments can help to redress the balance somewhat.

Before the liturgical reforms of the last century, a simplified form of ceremonial was used at masses for the dead which, among other things, stipulated that incense should not be used before the offertory, the Gospel Book should not be kissed at the end of the Gospel reading, and no one other than the celebrant should be censed at the offertory (for a more detailed description, see *Ritual Notes* 1946: pp. 586–95). None of these survived the reforms of the Second Vatican Council, and although there is certainly something to be said for creating an All Souls' liturgy which is stark in its simplicity, there are perhaps other ways in which this can be better achieved: for example, by the choice of music, use of silence and the pace at which the liturgy is celebrated.

Although only classified as a Lesser Festival in CW, TS provides a fully worked-out order of service for this Eucharist (TS: pp. 561–72) and, unlike other festivals of the same class, CW allows it to be transferred to the following day if 2 November falls on a Sunday (TS: p. 28).

The Gathering

The Gathering contains a minimal use of text. Appropriate words to introduce the penitential rite are suggested and two forms of penitence are provided. (The two absolutions which follow each other, one at the bottom of p. 543 and the other at the top of the following page, are meant to be alternative texts. Either may be used.) Although not printed in the text, the *Kyrie* may be said or sung before or after the absolution. The *Gloria in Excelsis* is not used on this occasion.

TS prefaces the collect with the following bidding: 'Let us pray for the peace and well-being of the whole Church.' Sensitive to differing opinions concerning prayer for the departed, it could not bring itself to invite prayer for, '. . . the whole Church, living and departed', although that would certainly be a suitable expansion of the bidding and provide a more obvious connection with the collect which follows. While the collect itself petitions the Father that we 'with all the faithful departed' may be granted 'the sure benefits of your Son's saving passion and glorious resurrection', for some a version which prays more explicitly for the departed would be more desirable. Such a prayer, based more closely on the original text from the 1928 Prayer Book, has been authorized by the Church in Wales. While lacking CW's reference to Christ's glorious resurrection, which could easily be inserted, this text may more adequately meet the need of those looking for more explicit prayer for the departed within the rite:

> Eternal God, our Maker and Redeemer,
> grant to all the faithful departed
> the sure benefits of your Son's saving passion,
> that, in the last day,
> when you gather up all things in Christ,
> they may enjoy the fullness of your promises;
> through Jesus Christ your Son our Lord . . .
> (Church in Wales 2003: p. 299)

Liturgy of the Word

As in other CW rites, one or two biblical readings may precede the Gospel reading. On this occasion, if the congregation includes a large number of visitors, and there are many names to read out within the commemoration of the departed, one reading may prove sufficient. As alternatives to those suggested in the lectionary, any of the readings commonly used at funerals would also be appropriate, as would Psalm 23, in one of its popular metrical versions, 'The Lord's my Shepherd' or 'The King of Love my Shepherd is'. Although TS provides the text for an Alleluia, if one of these hymns is used as a Gradual, it may be more appropriate to finish the hymn at the penultimate verse, read the Gospel, and then sing the final verse as the Gospel procession returns to the sanctuary.

Since there is no Creed on this occasion, the sermon, as well as setting the commemoration of the departed within the context of resurrection hope, can also function as a bridge between the proclamation of the Gospel and the Prayers of Intercession.

Although TS includes the Commemoration of the Faithful Departed, in which the names of the departed can be read aloud at the end of the service, after the Liturgy of the Sacrament and before the Dismissal, as Kennedy notes:

> While this structure works well, experience of using it suggests that the commemoration should not be excessive in terms of time or the service may lose some of its pastoral effectiveness by being *too* long or too over-loaded towards the end.
>
> (Kennedy 2006: p. 47)

With this in mind, he suggests a way in which the commemoration can be used at an earlier point in the service, as part of the intercession. While the overall balance of the service is certainly an important consideration, for those for whom prayer for the departed is central to their understanding of the commemoration of All Souls, it is most appropriate for the departed to be prayed for by name at the conclusion of the Prayers of Intercession. If the departed are commemorated at this juncture in the rite, immediately before the Liturgy of the Sacrament, the offering of the Eucharist for the repose of their souls is made more explicit.

Kennedy suggests a form of words which may added to the end of the intercessions provided, after which the names of the departed may be read: 'Jesus our hope, we remember in your presence those whom we love and see no longer' (Kennedy 2006: p. 47). To highlight this as a moment of prayer for the departed, the following may be preferred:

> Jesus, our resurrection and our life,
> grant us grace to entrust those whom we remember today
> to your never-failing love which sustained them in this life.
> Enfold them in the arms of your mercy, wipe away every tear
> from their eyes and receive them into your eternal kingdom.

The names of the departed are then read aloud. If there are many names, they may be shared between two or more people, including the clergy (and Readers) who usually officiate at funerals and, if the parish has a team of lay bereavement visitors, members of that group. It is important that the names are read clearly and not rushed. After the last name has been read an extended period of silence should be kept. Where musical resources permit, this may be followed by the Russian Contakion of the Departed, 'Give rest, O Christ, to your servants with your saints' (NEH 526), a version of the *Pie Jesu*, or another suitable chant, anthem or hymn, after which the president may conclude the commemoration with the prayer, 'Lord God, creator of all' (TS: p. 570) or 'Hear us, merciful Father' (TS: p. 571). During the hymn, members of the congregation could be invited to light candles in front of a Calvary, or in another suitable place, as a symbol of their remembrance of, and prayer for, departed loved ones.

The Liturgy of the Sacrament

TS suggests a short and extended preface which may be used in the Eucharistic Prayer. Both are quite triumphant in tone, proclaiming that 'the sting of death has been removed by the glorious promise of his risen life' and that 'the joy of the resurrection fills the universe'. For some who have been recently bereaved, a text which balances such confident assertions with an acknowledgement of the painful reality of death and grief may be pastorally more effective. For example, the following short preface from *Common Worship: Pastoral Services*:

> And now we give you thanks
> because through him you have given us
> the hope of a glorious resurrection;
> so that, although death comes to us all,
> yet we rejoice in the promise of eternal life;
> for to your faithful people life is changed, not taken away,
> and when our mortal flesh is laid aside
> an everlasting dwelling place is made ready for us in heaven.
> (PS: p. 283)

Not surprisingly, none of the CW Eucharistic Prayers contain petitions for the departed. Although stretching the bounds of canonical licence, some may wish to adapt the penultimate paragraph in Prayer B, incorporating material from Eucharistic Prayer III of the Roman Rite:

> Send the Holy Spirit on your people
> and gather into one in your kingdom
> all who share this one bread and one cup.
> Welcome into your kingdom our departed brothers and sisters
> and all who have left this world in your friendship.
> In the company of [*N and*] all the saints,
> may we with them praise and glorify you for ever,
> through Jesus Christ our Lord.

Even if not the text normally used on Sundays, the modified traditional version of the Lord's Prayer is probably most appropriate for this occasion, particularly if it is the one most commonly used at funerals. The special form of the *Agnus Dei*, which replaces *dona nobis pacem* (grant us peace) with *dona eis requiem* (grant them rest), is no longer required in masses for the dead, but may be considered appropriate. At the giving of Communion, these words of administration could be used in place of the usual formula:

> The bread of heaven in Christ Jesus.
> The cup of life in Christ Jesus.
> (CWMV: p. 295)

The Dismissal

If the commemoration of the departed has already taken place during the Prayers of Intercession, the service can end quite simply. Although no longer a feature of masses for the dead, the custom of replacing the blessing and dismissal with the following formula may be used:

President The Lord be with you
All **and also with you.**

President Let us bless the Lord.
All **Thanks be to God.**

President + May they rest in peace.
All **Amen.**

Remembrance Sunday

In the 1980s many people were predicting the demise of the observance of Remembrance Sunday, as the numbers of those who had lived through the two World Wars gradually decreased. Since that time, the involvement of the armed forces of the United Kingdom in conflicts in many parts of the world has reawakened the desire to hold an annual act of remembrance, which allows people of all ages to honour the dead, pray for those whose lives are scarred by war and terrorism, and commit themselves to working for peace and justice.

TS reproduces an Order of Service for Remembrance Sunday (TS: pp. 573–81), published in 2005, which was devised by a group convened by Churches Together in Britain and Ireland, working in co-operation with the Joint Liturgical Group and the Royal British Legion. Although this replaces the familiar ecumenical rite which had been in use since 1968, and which was reproduced in a slightly revised form in PHG, a number of texts from the 1968 order have been included in TS, and may be used at appropriate points in the 2005 service. Brian Elliott's collection of liturgies for remembrance, *They Shall Grow Not Old* (2006), contains both orders together with other resource material which is particularly suitable for Remembrance Sunday.

Table 4 A Service for Remembrance Sunday within the context of the Eucharist

CW Order 1 (2000)	*Service for Remembrance Sunday (2005)*
The Gathering	
Greeting	
	Sentences
	Introduction
Prayers of Penitence (TS: pp. 582–3)	
Collect	
Liturgy of the Word	
Readings	
Gospel	
Sermon	
Creed	
	Praying Together
	Remembering
Liturgy of the Sacrament	
Peace (TS: p. 585)	
Offertory	
Eucharistic Prayer	
Lord's Prayer	
Breaking of the Bread	
Giving of Communion	
Prayer after Communion	
Responding in Hope and Commitment	
	Kohima Epitaph
	Act of Commitment
	National Anthem
	Blessing
Dismissal	

In PHG the Liturgical Commission suggested ways in which the 1968 order could be combined with a celebration of the Eucharist or Morning or Evening Prayer. Although the 2005 revision contains a number of detailed notes concerning the celebration of the rite, it is regrettable that there is no outline order showing how it might be used at the Eucharist. Although the order will depend partly on the time of the service, and when and where the act of remembrance is to take place, one possibility is set out here. Rather than placing the act of remembrance at the beginning of the service (which feels rather odd, since this is in some sense the climax of the rite), it has been included as part of the Prayers of Intercession, but may, of course, be used at another appropriate point. (See Table 4.)

The liturgical colour should be green or red, whichever is used from All Saints to Advent. Although some communities celebrate a Requiem on Remembrance Sunday, in purple or black vestments, since every Sunday is, first and foremost, a celebration of the resurrection, this is not appropriate, at least not at the principal service of the day. Many of the readings appointed for use on the Third and Second Sundays before Advent are well suited to Remembrance Sunday. However, if desired, other suitable readings, such as those listed in note 6 (TS: p. 574), may replace them. When Remembrance Sunday falls on the Second Sunday before Advent, its collect and post-Communion prayer may be swapped with that for the Third Sunday before Advent, which is more appropriate for this occasion (see MV: pp. 496–7).

Christ the King

The Feast of Christ the King was introduced into the Roman Catholic Calendar by Pope Pius XI in 1925. Originally observed on the last Sunday of October, since 1970 it has been kept on the Sunday next before Advent, thus bringing the liturgical year to a conclusion with a triumphant celebration of Christ's universal lordship over heaven and earth. First trialled in the Church of England in PHG, it was officially introduced into the calendar in 1997.

CW suggests red or white as the liturgical colour for this feast. Even if red has been used in the preceding weeks, white is the more usual colour for feasts of our Lord (for example, the Naming and Circumcision of Jesus on 1 January and the Transfiguration on

6 August). White also enables a mirroring of the Festival of All Saints which, in the CW calendar, begins this final period of Ordinary Time.

TS does not provide a complete order for the Eucharist on this Sunday, but rather provides a selection of textual resources which may be used. There is no distinctive ceremonial for this festival, but a procession round the church, as described above for the Eucharist of All Saints, would certainly be appropriate. In some communities it is customary to conclude this Eucharist with a procession of the Blessed Sacrament and Benediction.

7

Daily prayer and initiation rites through the year

Daily prayer

Blessed are you, Lord our God.
How sweet are your words to the taste,
sweeter than honey to the mouth.
How precious are your commands for our life,
more than the finest gold in our hands.
How marvellous is your will for the world,
unending is your love for the nations.
Our voices shall sing of your promises
and our lips declare your praise.
Blessed be God, Father, Son and Holy Spirit.
Blessed be God for ever.

(Prayer of Thanksgiving from
Thanksgiving for the Word, DP, p. 304)

While this volume relates primarily to the liturgical material contained in TS, the creative celebration of the Christian year should also affect the way in which other rites are used and, not least, daily prayer. One of the most distinctive features of DP, as compared with the BCP and ASB, is the possibility of celebrating both the *Temporale* and the *Sanctorale* with a degree of richness hitherto unknown in the Church of England.

Influenced by *Celebrating Common Prayer* (1992), the product of a semi-official partnership between members of the Liturgical Commission and the Society of St Francis, DP provides complete seasonal forms of Prayer During the Day, Morning Prayer and Evening Prayer, together with a number of seasonal variations for use with the standard form of Night Prayer. These forms, together with other supplementary material, allow the text of the office to relate to particular seasons through the appropriate use of biblical and post-biblical canticles, hymns, responsories, refrains, forms of intercession and collects, not to mention the psalmody and readings contained in the Sunday and weekday lectionaries. When considering how to use this wealth of material, it is worth bearing in mind Cranmer's complaint concerning the medieval office, that it could sometimes take longer to find out what to pray on a particular occasion than to pray it! Faced with such an embarrassment of riches, it is important that the contemporary office does not become overly complex, or the use of material proper to a particular commemoration detract from the continuous celebration of a season.

To this end, note 5 (DP: p. 411) makes clear that, on Lesser Festivals, the use of a common refrain with the Gospel canticle is optional. As with alternative canticles, it is likely that they will only be appropriate if, for some reason, a Lesser Festival is being observed as a Festival or Principal Feast, as, for example, on a Patronal Festival. The provision of a refrain for the *Magnificat* on the eve of a Festival is also optional, and is only likely to be needed on a Saturday evening, or if the Festival is being kept as a Principal Feast, when a 'First Evensong' should be celebrated.

The seasonal notes (DP: pp. xv–xvi) explain the duration of each season and give some guidance on how they might be celebrated within the context of daily prayer, but there is also much to be said for considering the appropriate use of space and symbol to enhance the celebration of the Christian year by communities and individuals praying the daily office. What follows is not intended to be prescriptive, but rather to encourage creative consideration of what might be possible.

Advent

In Advent, during Evening Prayer, the movement from darkness to light could be symbolized by the lighting of candles on the Advent Wreath. This could take place during the *Lucernarium*, the Blessing of Light (DP: pp. 110–11), which replaces the Preparation at the beginning of the service. Occasionally, instead of using the thanksgiving prayer provided in the Advent order (DP: p. 205), it may be appropriate to use one of those in TS which give thanks for those groups and individuals who prepared for the coming of Christ: the Patriarchs, the Prophets, John the Baptist and the Blessed Virgin Mary (TS: pp. 51–4). If, on some days, a penitential introduction to the morning or evening office is desired, the Prayers of Penitence at the Advent Wreath (TS, pp. 56-7) would be a suitable alternative to the penitential forms provided in DP (pp. 91–7).

From 17 to 23 December the 'Great O' antiphons (DP: p. 211; TS: pp. 58–9) are said or sung before and after the *Magnificat*. TS suggests that these may be used as the framework for an extended liturgical meditation, and it may be appropriate to encourage members of the community to attend Evening Prayer on these days as a final act of preparation before Christmas, even if they are not part of a group which regularly prays the office together. An alternative lectionary (TS: p. 59), based on the Advent Antiphons, is also provided for use at Evening Prayer on these days.

Christmas

During the 12 days of Christmas, and from Epiphany to the eve of the Baptism of Christ, those saying the office in church could gather round the crib. If Evening Prayer begins with the Blessing of Light, candles placed either side of the crib could be lit and, if incense is used, it could be burnt in a bowl in front of the crib, as well as during the *Magnificat*.

Epiphany

The Feast of the Baptism of Christ would be an appropriate occasion to use the Thanksgiving for Holy Baptism (DP: pp. 306–7), particularly if the Eucharist on that day has not included the renewal of baptismal vows and sprinkling with baptismal water. Prayers for the Unity of the Church (pp. 315–16) could be used during the Week of Prayer for Christian Unity (18–25 January), and the Thanksgiving for the Mission of the Church (pp. 312–14) would also be appropriate in the weeks before the Presentation. Like the Thanksgiving for Holy Baptism, it is probably better suited to a Sunday Service of the Word than a weekday office.

Lent

It is desirable that, during Lent, the normal pattern of praying the office is simplified. The Acclamation of Christ at the Dawning of the Day and Blessing of Light are less suited to this season. A penitential rite may begin the office, particularly on Fridays, and it would also be appropriate for the Litany to be said, at least weekly, during the season. If two readings are normally used at Morning and/or Evening Prayer, these could be reduced to one, and followed by a lengthy period of silence. The Prayers at the Foot of the Cross (DP: pp. 317–18) could also be used weekly, perhaps on a Friday evening. If a church has its own Calvary, which is used as a focus for devotion throughout the year, it would be appropriate to gather there for these prayers and for candles to be lit in front of it. Incense could also be burned in a bowl as the prayers are offered.

Passiontide

In Passiontide, the congregation could gather round such a Calvary or another cross or crucifix for the whole of the office. If it is the custom to veil crosses during this season, it may be appropriate to drape the veil over the arms of this cross, so that it is not completely obscured. During the Triduum, the office should be celebrated as simply as possible with extended periods of silence. Note 4 (DP: p. xx) explains how this may be done.

Easter

Parallel to the crib at Christmas, many churches build an Easter Garden to celebrate the resurrection of Christ. During the Easter octave those praying the office could gather around it. A bowl of baptismal water could be placed near it and, following the custom in some monastic communities at the end of Compline, the congregation could be sprinkled with it, or sign themselves with it, at the end of Evening (or Night) Prayer. Alternatively, to express union with the disciples whom Christ greeted after his resurrection, the Peace may be exchanged at the conclusion of the service (DP: p. xviii, note 9).

The Paschal Candle provides the principal symbolic focus

throughout the season. It should be lit at all services between Easter and Pentecost and, if possible, be visible to those saying the office, whether or not they gather around it. In some churches it may be possible to place it next to the lectern or legilium, so that the light of the risen Christ illuminates the reading of the Word of God. At Evening Prayer, it could be lit during the Blessing of Light, and its light used to light other candles. If incense is used, it could be burned in front of the Candle and, again, at the *Magnificat*. On Saturday evenings during Eastertide the Vigil Office is particularly appropriate (DP: pp. 325–30). Hand-held candles could be lit from the Paschal Candle during the Blessing of Light and remain lit throughout the service. If that is not practical, they could be lit before the Sunday Gospel is proclaimed. TS also suggests that the Thanksgiving for the Resurrection (TS: pp. 421–4) could be used as a Processional at Evening Prayer.

At Morning Prayer, the Acclamation of Christ at the Dawning of the Day is particularly suited to this season as is, on Sundays, the Commemoration of the Resurrection (DP: pp. 319–24), though this will probably not bear repetition on each of the Sundays of Easter. For some, the place where the Blessed Sacrament is reserved will be an appropriate location for Morning Prayer, as those who gather worship the risen Christ who made himself known in the breaking of the bread.

Although part of Eastertide, DP provides separate orders for the period from Ascension Day to Pentecost, so that thanksgiving for the resurrection can give way to prayer for the coming of the Spirit. Simple chants, such as *Veni, sancte Spiritus*, from the Taizé community, may be sung before the service, in place of the responsory, or during the prayers.

All Saints to Advent

In the period from All Saints' Day to Advent, for which DP gives another order, icons of the saints may be put in a prominent position within the liturgical space, with a red (or blue, for the Blessed Virgin Mary) lamp burning in front of them. If incense is used, they may be censed during the *Magnificat*, or incense may be burnt in front of them during the prayers. TS suggests that the Litany of Thanksgiving for the Holy Ones of God may be used at Morning or

Evening Prayer during All Saints' tide (TS: pp. 558–9). Replacing the prayers, it could be used in procession round the church.

Festivals

Moving from the *Temporale* to the *Sanctorale*, appropriate icons may also be used on feasts of the Blessed Virgin Mary, the apostles and other saints. DP suggests that, at Morning and Evening Prayer, the celebration of Festivals may be further enriched by the optional use of different seasonal orders to accompany particular observances. Note 3 (DP: p. 104) lists these, and there is a further note to this effect beneath the title of each Festival to which it applies. Thus, for example, the Christmas orders may be used on Festivals of the Blessed Virgin Mary, and the Passiontide orders on Holy Cross Day. Appropriate alternative canticles are also suggested to replace those within the main orders, including the use of the *Te Deum* at Morning Prayer on feasts of apostles and evangelists. Non-biblical, hagiographical readings may also enhance the celebration of the *Sanctorale*. Various collections of these are readily available, including Robert Atwell's *Celebrating the Saints* (1998) and those appointed for the Office of Readings in the Roman breviary. If used at Morning and Evening Prayer, they may be read before the beginning of the service, or following the responsory, in the place where a sermon may be preached (DP: p. 105, note 8).

On Sundays, Principal Feasts and Festivals, it may be appropriate to celebrate the offices more elaborately than on other occasions. Exactly how this is done will depend on a number of factors, not least the musical resources available, the layout and size of the liturgical space, and the number of people present. *Ritual Notes* provides the ceremonial for Solemn Evensong, and this remains part of the worshipping pattern of a number of communities. Where it is desired to provide a 'solemn' or festal form of one of the offices in DP, the officiant could wear a cope of the colour of the day. At Evening Prayer, the order could begin with the Blessing of Light, during which the Paschal Candle (in Eastertide), altar candles and other lamps and candles could be lit by acolytes or others. As verses from Psalm 141 are said or sung, incense could be burned in a bowl or censer, placed on or near the altar, or in some other suitable place. Where possible, the psalms and canticles should be sung, if necessary using metrical forms. At the Gospel Canticle, the altar, officiant and congregation could be censed or, alternatively, more incense could be burnt in a bowl. When the (perhaps Solemn) *Te Deum* or *Gloria in Excelsis* is used as a canticle of praise immediately before the Conclusion to Morning Prayer (DP: p. 107, note 15), incense could again be burnt, or the thurifer, facing the altar, could swing the thurible across the body. At a Vigil Office, the Gospel Book could be censed before the Gospel of the Sunday or festival is proclaimed, and acolytes could stand either side of the reader, as at the Eucharist.

Initiation services

> And now we give you thanks
> because by water and the Holy Spirit
> you have made us a holy people in Jesus Christ our Lord,
> you raise us to new life in him
> and renew in us the image of your glory.
> (Short Preface for Baptism and Confirmation, CI: p. 160)

The celebration of baptism as the centre point around which is clustered a series of accompanied, staged rites is fundamental to CW's theology of Christian initiation. The theological, liturgical and missiological rationale for this 'catechumenate model' of initiation is outlined in the introduction to CI. CW makes clear that these Rites on the Way, which accompany a candidate's journey towards baptism and, afterwards, assist the candidate to appropriate the ethical and spiritual characteristics of the baptismal life, are 'most appropriately celebrated by the whole community when placed within particular sections of the cycle of the Christian year' (CI: pp. 5–6). Three are mentioned: the Epiphany/Baptism of Christ; Easter/Pentecost; and All Saints' tide. Later in the volume, further justification is given to this seasonal approach:

> Rites on the Way support a journey of faith which in some ways mirrors the story of Jesus as it is told by the Christian community through the seasons. It is therefore appropriate to use the seasons to enhance the sense of journey and of the climax to that journey which is already firmly within the historical understanding of the faith.
>
> (CI: p. 330)

It is not for this guide to provide a detailed commentary on these rites. For that, see chapter 6 in CCW2. CI itself provides some helpful notes on 'seasonal patterns of initiation for those who can answer for themselves' (pp. 330–2), but these relate mainly to how the various rites might be distributed within the three seasons mentioned above. In this chapter our concern is how their use within particular seasons might affect the way in which they are celebrated, with particular reference to the Call and Celebration of the Decision to be Baptized or Confirmed or to Affirm Baptismal Faith (CI: pp. 37–9) and the celebration of baptism and confirmation (CI: pp. 59–179).

Call and Celebration of the Decision to be Baptized or Confirmed or to Affirm Baptismal Faith

Intended for use within an act of public worship, three positions are permitted for the Call and Celebration of the Decision to be Baptized, Confirmed or Affirm Baptismal Faith: before the collect, after the sermon or before the peace (CI: p. 37, note 2). If initiation is celebrated at Easter (either at the Vigil or on Easter Day), CI suggests that the liturgical celebration of the decision to make this step may take place on the First Sunday of Lent; if the Feast of the Epiphany or of the Baptism of Christ is the occasion for initiation, the Call may take place on the First Sunday of Advent; if All Saints' Day or All Saints' Sunday, then the Decision may be celebrated on the Feast of the Holy Cross (14 September) or the Sunday nearest to it.

On the First Sunday of Lent or of Advent, it may be particularly appropriate for the Call and Celebration to take place immediately following the Prayers of Penitence. To highlight the link with baptism, the ministers could process to the font (if it is visible to the assembly) during the first half of a hymn or song or, if musical resources permit, as verses from the Lent or Advent Prose are sung. The introduction could be incorporated into words of welcome following the greeting, which could lead into the penitential rite. For example, on the First Sunday of Lent:

(Following the Greeting)

Today it is our joy and privilege to welcome *N* and *N*,
disciples with us on the Way of Christ.
They are among us as sign of the journey of faith
to which we are all called.
As we commit ourselves to supporting them
let us confess with them the ways
in which we have failed to take up our cross and follow Christ
on the way that leads to life.

The Prayers of Penitence follow, including a period of silence, confession and absolution, after which the president could invite the candidates to leave their places and stand before the congregation for the question, signing with the cross, presentation of a Gospel and prayers for the candidates. The opening hymn or song could then be concluded as the ministers process to the altar, the candidates accompanying them and taking their place with their sponsors at the front of the assembly. If incense is used, the altar could be censed at this point, and the service continue with the collect and Liturgy of the Word.

On Holy Cross Day, or the Sunday nearest to it (when red could be used as the liturgical colour with the collect, readings and propers of the feast), it would be appropriate for a large cross or crucifix to be the focus for the Gathering. This might be a Calvary which is a permanent fixture in the church, or a large cross might be set up especially for the occasion, perhaps near the font. As in Lent/Advent, words of welcome and introduction could be combined and lead into the penitential rite. After a Gospel is presented, candidates might also be given a small icon of the patron saint of the church, of the Blessed Virgin Mary, or one of the other saints commemorated in the building, to symbolize their being 'surrounded by so great a cloud of witnesses' (Hebrews 12.1) on their journey which will reach a significant staging-point on the Feast of All Saints. Before the Prayers of Intercession are offered, the prayers of the saints and of the community supporting the candidates might also be symbolized by the sponsors spooning incense into a bowl of charcoal set up in front of the cross.

Whenever this rite is celebrated, whatever additional symbolism is employed, it should not detract from the central act of signing candidates with the cross on the forehead. Note 3 (CI: p. 37) permits the use of oil for this purpose which, for those preparing for baptism, should be the Oil of Catechumens. For candidates who are already baptized, a separate formula is provided which acknowledges that they have already been 'claimed' by Christ 'for his own'. Although CI also permits these candidates to be anointed, the use of the Oil of Catechumens within the tradition has, as its name suggests, been confined to those preparing for baptism, and there seems to be little justification for departing from that. Moreover, to distinguish visually as well as verbally between candidates who have been baptized and those who are preparing for baptism, seems helpful at this point in the rite. For further discussion regarding the use of oil in this service, as well as in baptism and confirmation, see chapter 3 of *The Use of Symbols in Worship* (ALG 4, 2007).

Baptism and confirmation

CI contains extensive seasonal provision for baptism and confirmation (pp. 150–65) and suggests that material for use at Epiphany and on the Feast of the Baptism of Christ is also appropriate on Trinity Sunday. For each of the three seasonal periods there are words to introduce the rite, an acclamation at the Blessing of Light (from DP, for use when initiation is celebrated at a Vigil Service), a collect, suggested Bible readings and psalms, a Gospel acclamation, a prayer over the water, a form of intercession, an introduction to the Peace, eucharistic prefaces, a post-Communion prayer and a blessing.

While this material, appropriately used, helps to weave seasonal themes throughout the rite, care needs to be taken that it does not overload the celebration with texts, particularly if a significant proportion of those present are not familiar with the proliferation of biblical images which they contain. For example, a simpler, more informal introduction to the service may be a more effective way of preparing people for what is about to happen than some of the richer, carefully crafted forms in CI. The appropriateness of responsive forms of prayer over the water also needs to be considered. Though intended to increase congregational participation, their use requires a full text to be printed in the order of service, thus preventing visual engagement with what is happening at this central moment in the rite. A detailed commentary on the CW rites of baptism and confirmation can be found in chapter 7 of CCW1.

If candidates have been preparing during Lent, it is most suitable for them to be baptized and/or confirmed at the Easter Vigil. This rite is discussed in detail in the next volume of this series. When there are celebrations of Christian initiation on Easter Day, or other Sundays of Easter, it may be appropriate for the Paschal Candle to replace the processional cross in the entrance procession. Carried by a deacon or other minister, candidates and their sponsors may follow it in the procession before taking their place at the front of the assembly. When the candidates, sponsors and ministers move to the font, the Litany of the Resurrection (CI: pp. 172–3) may be said or sung, and the Paschal Candle should lead them there and back. When candles are given to the candidates at the end of the rite, they should be lit from the Paschal Candle which, once its light has been shared with them, need not lead them through the church at the end of the service.

If initiation is celebrated on the Festival of the Baptism of Christ, it follows the Liturgy of the Word and replaces the Thanksgiving for Holy Baptism provided in TS. A full outline of the rite (with or without baptism) can be found in TS (pp. 170–1). On this feast, it may be appropriate for a large ewer of water to be carried in the entrance procession in front of the candidates and their sponsors, who may precede the ministers. The vessel of water may also be carried at the head of the procession to the font, and poured into the font by one of the sponsors. If a hymn is sung at the beginning of the Dismissal (TS: pp. 182–3), it would be appropriate for the ministers, candidates and their sponsors to process again to the font, the congregation turning towards them, for the acclamation, dismissal Gospel and blessing. Where this is done, it will be possible for the baptismal candles to be lit from the Paschal Candle before they are presented.

If initiation is celebrated as part of the Eucharist of All Saints (TS: pp. 548–57), the candidates and their sponsors could precede the ministers in the entrance procession, making a station at a statue, icon, or other image of the church's patron saint, or of the Blessed Virgin Mary. A prayer of thanksgiving, such as that in DP (p. 257) or

CI (p. 161), could be said, preferably by a minister other than the president. The candidates could light candles before the image, in thanksgiving for the prayers of the saints and of the local community which have accompanied them on their journey, and the president could cense the image before the procession continues. Within the Gathering, the Prayers of Penitence should be omitted, and the Presentation of the Candidates may take place before the *Gloria* (or Beatitudes). The Liturgy of Initiation follows the sermon (the Creed is omitted), and the Thanksgiving for the Holy Ones of God (TS: pp. 558–60) may appropriately be used for the procession to and from the font. At the end of the rite, the Dismissal may also be celebrated at the font, as already suggested for the Feast of the Baptism of Christ.

Vigil services

CI also provides material for the celebration of baptism and confirmation within a Vigil Service (CI: pp. 132–49) which may be used on the Eve of the Baptism of Christ or on Saturdays in Epiphany, on Saturdays in Eastertide, and on the Eve of All Saints' Day or on Saturdays between All Saints and Advent Sunday. It is an episcopal service which is most likely to be celebrated when there are a significant number of candidates, either as a diocesan service in the cathedral, or as a deanery service in a large parish church. In the way it is constructed, it can only be used if there are candidates for baptism *and* confirmation. If the bishop wears cope and mitre, it would be appropriate for the deacon to wear a matching dalmatic.

The service begins in darkness with a *Lucernarium*. Verses from Isaiah 43, read from the lectern or pulpit by the light of a torch or from behind the people, are likely to be more effective than the responsory which requires the congregation to be able to see the order of service. The large candle which is lit at the Blessing of Light will, in most contexts, be the Paschal Candle, which should be placed in a prominent position so that it can be clearly seen. If it is placed in front of the pulpit, it would be appropriate for the deacon to say the thanksgiving prayer from the pulpit.

The way in which the rite is celebrated will depend on the layout of the building, the number of candidates to be baptized and/or confirmed and the space available. A ewer of water may be carried in the procession to the font, and poured into the font by one of the sponsors. To highlight the proclamation of the Gospel, the Gospel Book may be censed, as at the Eucharist, or incense may be burnt in a bowl in front of the lectern or legilium. Afterwards, it would be appropriate for the bishop to kiss the book and bless the congregation with it. At the end of the rite, a simple greeting followed by the responses which traditionally precede an episcopal blessing (see note 13, CI: p. 130) could be used. At the Dismissal, although double alleluias are suggested, their use is normally restricted to the Easter season to preserve their distinctiveness, and so they are perhaps less appropriate at other times of the year.

Sources

Texts

Celebrating Common Prayer (London: Mowbray, 1992).

Celebrating the Easter Mystery: Worship Resources for Easter to Pentecost (London: Mowbray, 1996).

The Christian Year: Calendar, Lectionary and Collects (London: Church House Publishing, 1997).

Common Worship: Christian Initiation (London: Church House Publishing, 2006).

Common Worship: Daily Prayer (London: Church House Publishing, 2005).

Common Worship: Festivals (London: Church House Publishing, 2008).

Common Worship: Pastoral Services (London: Church House Publishing, 2000).

Common Worship: Services and Prayers for the Church of England (London: Church House Publishing, 2000).

Common Worship: Services and Prayers for the Church of England: President's Edition (London: Church House Publishing, 2000).

Common Worship: Times and Seasons (London: Church House Publishing, 2006).

Elliott, Brian, *They Shall Grow Not Old* (Norwich: Canterbury Press, 2006).

Enriching the Christian Year, ed. Michael Perham et al. (London: SPCK/Alcuin Club, 1993).

Enriching the Liturgy, ed. J. P. Young (London: SPCK, 1998).

Griffiths, Alan, *Celebrating the Christian Year*, 3 vols (Norwich: Canterbury Press, 2004–5).

Hymns Old & New, New Anglican Edition (Great Wakering: Kevin Mayhew, 1996).

Lent, Holy Week, Easter: Services and Prayers (London: CHP/CUP/SPCK, 1986).

The Methodist Worship Book (Peterborough: Methodist Publishing House, 1999).

The New English Hymnal (Norwich: Canterbury Press, 1986).

New English Praise (Norwich: Canterbury Press, 2006).
New Patterns for Worship (London: Church House Publishing, 2002).
The Promise of His Glory: Services and Prayers for the Season from All Saints to Candlemas (London: Mowbray/Church House Publishing, 1991).
The Sunday Missal (London: HarperCollins, 2005).
The Weekday Missal (London: Collins, 1982).

Studies, guides and other works

Anglican Services: A Book Concerning Ritual and Ceremonial in the Church of England (London: W. Knott & Son, 1953).
Atwell, Robert, *Celebrating the Saints* (Norwich: Canterbury Press, 1998).
Bradshaw, Paul, ed., *Companion to Common Worship Vol. 1*, Alcuin Club Collection 78 (London: SPCK, 2001).
Bradshaw, Paul, ed., *Companion to Common Worship Vol. 2*, Alcuin Club Collection 81 (London: SPCK, 2006).
Bradshaw, Paul, ed., *The New SCM Dictionary of Liturgy and Worship* (London: SCM, 2002).
Casel, O., *Das Christliche Festmysterium* (Paderborn: Bonifacius, 1941).
Casel, O., *The Mystery of Christian Worship*, tr. B. Neuenheuser (London: Darton, Longman & Todd, 1962).
Church in Wales, *The Book of Common Prayer for use in the Church of Wales: The New Calendar and The Collects* (Norwich: Canterbury Press, 2003).
Cooke, B., 'Sacraments', in *A New Dictionary of Sacramental Worship*, ed. P. Fink (Collegeville, MN: Liturgical Press, 1990), pp. 1116-22.
Cowley, Patrick, *Advent: Its Liturgical Significance* (London: Faith Press, 1960).
Dean, Stephen, ed., *The Great Week* (McCrimmons, 1992).
Dearmer, Percy, *The Parson's Handbook*, 12th edition (London: Oxford University Press, 1932).
Denis-Boulet, N.M., *The Christian Calendar* (London: Burns & Oates, 1960).
A Directory of Ceremonial, Part II, Alcuin Club Tracts XIX, second edition (London: Mowbray, 1950).
Donne, John, *The Complete English Poems*, ed. A. J. Smith (London: Penguin, 1971).
Dunlop, Colin, *Processions: A Dissertation Together With Practical Suggestions*, Alcuin Club Tracts XX (London: Mowbray, 1932).
Earey, M., Lloyd, T., Moger, P. and Stratford, T., *Introducing Times and*

Seasons 1: The Christmas Cycle, Grove Worship Series 189 (Cambridge: Grove Books, 2006).

Elliott, Peter J., *Ceremonies of the Liturgical Year According to the Modern Roman Rite* (San Francisco: Ignatius Press, 2002).

Foley, E., Mitchell, N. D. and Pierce, J. M., eds, *A Commentary on the General Instruction of the Roman Missal* (Collegeville, MN: Liturgical Press, 2007).

Fortescue, Adrian and O'Connell, J., *The Ceremonies of the Roman Rite Described*, 8th edition further revised (London: Burns Oates and Washbourne, 1948).

Galley, Howard E, *The Ceremonies of the Eucharist: A Guide to Celebration* (Cambridge, MA: Cowley Publications, 1989).

General Instruction of the Roman Missal (London: Catholic Truth Society, 2005).

Hooker, R., *Of the Laws of Ecclesiastical Polity*, V, lxix, in *The Works of Mr. Richard Hooker*, 2v. (Oxford: Clarendon Press, 1890), Vol. 2.

Hutchinson, F. E., ed., *The Works of George Herbert* (Oxford: Clarendon Press, 1941).

Irwin, Kevin W., *Advent and Christmas: A Guide to the Eucharist and Hours* (New York: Pueblo, 1986).

Kavanagh, A., *On Liturgical Theology* (Collegeville, MN: Liturgical Press, 1992).

Kennedy, David, *Using Common Worship: Times and Seasons All Saints to Candlemas* (London: Church House Publishing, 2006).

Lloyd, T., Sinclair, J. and Vasey, M., *Introducing Promise of His Glory*, Grove Worship Series 116 (Bramcote: Grove Books, 1991).

Mackenzie, K. D., *The Way of the Church*, 4th edition (London: Mowbray, 1956).

Merton, Thomas, 'The Sacrament of Advent in the Spirituality of St Bernard', in *Seasons of Celebration* (New York: Farrar, Straus & Giroux, 1965), pp. 61–87.

Merton, Thomas, *Meditations on Liturgy* (London: Mowbray, 1976).

Michno, D., *A Priest's Handbook: the Ceremonies of the Church* (New York: Morehouse, 1998).

More, P. E. and Cross, F. L., eds, *Anglicanism: The Thought and Practice of the Church of England, Illustrated from the Religious Literature of the Seventeenth Century* (London: SPCK, 1935).

Perham, Michael and Stevenson, Kenneth, *Welcoming the Light of Christ: A Commentary on The Promise of His Glory* (London: SPCK, 1991).

Ritual Notes (London: W. Knott & Son, 1946, 1947 and 1956).

St Bernard On The Christian Year, ed. A Religious of CSMV (London: Mowbray, 1954).

Silk, David, *Prayers for Use at the Alternative Services* (London: Mowbray, 1986).

Stevenson, Kenneth, *All the Company of Heaven: a Companion to the Principal Festivals of the Christian Year* (Norwich: Canterbury Press, 1998).

Stevenson, Kenneth, *Watching and Waiting: A Guide to the Celebration of Advent* (Norwich: Canterbury Press, 2007).

Talley, Thomas, *The Origins of the Liturgical Year* (New York: Pueblo, 1986).

Wright, Geoffrey, *Living Traditions* (London: Church Union, 1994).

Index